AF344254

Language and Globalization

Series Editors: **Sue Wright**, University of Portsmouth, UK and **Helen Kelly-Holmes**, University of Limerick, Ireland.

In the context of current political and social developments, where the national group is not so clearly defined and delineated, the state language not so clearly dominant in every domain, and cross-border flows and transfers affect more than a small elite, new patterns of language use will develop. The series aims to provide a framework for reporting on and analysing the linguistic outcomes of globalization and localization.

Titles include:

David Block
MULTILINGUAL IDENTITIES IN A GLOBAL CITY
London Stories

Jenny Carl and Patrick Stevenson (*editors*)
LANGUAGE, DISCOURSE AND IDENTITY IN CENTRAL EUROPE
The German Language in a Multilingual Space

Diarmait Mac Giolla Chríost
LANGUAGE AND THE CITY

Julian Edge (*editor*)
(RE)LOCATING TESOL IN AN AGE OF EMPIRE

Aleksandra Galasińska and Michał Krzyżanowski (*editors*)
DISCOURSE AND TRANSFORMATION IN CENTRAL AND EASTERN EUROPE

Roxy Harris
NEW ETHNICITIES AND LANGUAGE USE

Jane Jackson
INTERCULTURAL JOURNEYS
From Study to Residence Abroad

Helen Kelly-Holmes and Gerlinde Mautner (*editors*)
LANGUAGE AND THE MARKET

Clare Mar-Molinero and Patrick Stevenson (*editors*)
LANGUAGE IDEOLOGIES, POLICIES AND PRACTICES
Language and the Future of Europe

Clare Mar-Molinero and Miranda Stewart (*editors*)
GLOBALIZATION AND LANGUAGE IN THE SPANISH-SPEAKING WORLD
Macro and Micro Perspectives

Ulrike Hanna Meinhof and Dariusz Galasinski
THE LANGUAGE OF BELONGING

Richard C. M. Mole (*editor*)
DISCURSIVE CONSTRUCTIONS OF IDENTITY IN EUROPEAN POLITICS

Leigh Oakes and Jane Warren
LANGUAGE, CITIZENSHIP AND IDENTITY IN QUEBEC

Mario Saraceni
THE RELOCATION OF ENGLISH
Shifting Paradigms in a Global Era

Christina Slade and Martina Mollering (*editors*)
FROM MIGRANT TO CITIZEN: TESTING LANGUAGE, TESTING CULTURE

Colin Williams
LINGUISTIC MINORITIES IN DEMOCRATIC CONTEXT

Forthcoming titles:

John Edwards
CHALLENGES IN THE SOCIAL LIFE OF LANGUAGE

Language and Globalization
Series Standing Order ISBN 978–1–4039–9731–9 Hardback
978–1–4039–9732–6 Paperback
(*outside North America only*)

You can receive future titles in this series as they are published by placing a standing order. Please contact your bookseller or, in case of difficulty, write to us at the address below with your name and address, the title of the series and the ISBN quoted above.

Customer Services Department, Macmillan Distribution Ltd, Houndmills, Basingstoke, Hampshire RG21 6XS, England

---

The Relocation of English

Shifting Paradigms in a Global Era

Mario Saraceni
University of Portsmouth, UK

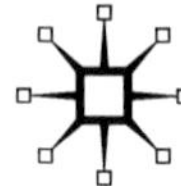

First published 2010 by
PALGRAVE MACMILLAN

Palgrave Macmillan in the UK is an imprint of Macmillan Publishers Limited, registered in England, company number 785998, of Houndmills, Basingstoke, Hampshire RG21 6XS.

Palgrave Macmillan in the US is a division of St Martin's Press LLC, 175 Fifth Avenue, New York, NY 10010.

Palgrave Macmillan is the global academic imprint of the above companies and has companies and representatives throughout the world.

Palgrave® and Macmillan® are registered trademarks in the United States, the United Kingdom, Europe and other countries.

ISBN-13: 978–0–230–20665–6 hardback

This book is printed on paper suitable for recycling and made from fully managed and sustained forest sources. Logging, pulping and manufacturing processes are expected to conform to the environmental regulations of the country of origin.

A catalogue record for this book is available from the British Library.

A catalog record for this book is available from the Library of Congress.

10   9   8   7   6   5   4   3   2   1
19 18 17 16 15 14 13 12 11 10

Printed and bound in Great Britain by
CPI Antony Rowe, Chippenham and Eastbourne

To Marta, for her immense patience

Contents

List of Figures and Tables

Figures

Tables

Acknowledgements

I would not have been able to write this book without the direct or indirect help, support and advice given to me by a long list of people over the last 3 years. While it would be impossible for me to mention every one of them, I would like to express my gratitude to the following individuals:

It was first of and foremost thanks to Sue Wright, my colleague, mentor and source of endless inspiration, that I was able to embark on this project. Her advice and criticism throughout the writing process have been absolutely vital.

I must also thank Jill Lake, former commissioning editor at Palgrave, for believing in this book when it was only an idea.

My gratitude goes to Ganakumaran Subramaniam, my old-time friend and colleague, for inviting me to spend part of my sabbatical at Universiti Kebangsaan Malaysia and facilitating my data collection. My thanks are extended to all his colleagues at UKM who helped me during my stay there.

While writing this book I occasionally sought advice from scholars whose expertise I value immensely: I am indebted to E. Annamalai, Jennifer Jenkins, John Joseph and Margie Berns for being extremely kind in answering my queries.

I would also like to thank my friend and colleague Richard Hitchcock, for taking the time to read parts of the manuscript and offering invaluable comments.

Finally, I could not possibly fail to mention the generous and enthusiastic assistance provided by all the Malaysian students who have taken part in my survey, both in Malaysia and in the UK.

Preface

Research, and academic activity in general, is always spurred by some initial intuition and curiosity about a particular state of affairs. This book is no exception. In this preface I would like to recount three anecdotes that, to some extent, illustrate my own initial intuitions and act as the incipit to the discussion that ensues in the chapters that follow.

Anecdote 1

Luang Prabang is a small town in Laos whose artistic and natural beauty has in recent years attracted a growing number of travellers, especially after the opening of an international airport. One evening, when I visited the town, I was having something to eat at a typical Southeast Asian outdoor food stall very popular with international travellers. It was normal that there would be about 20 or 30 people of different nationalities eating and talking together. English was used as a lingua franca and conversations were smooth. The owner of the place would occasionally join in while dishing out the food. On that particular evening, while things were proceeding in the usual jovial manner, there was a curious incident of linguistic misunderstanding when a freshly graduated Englishman asked the owner for some 'plain water'. The owner looked at his customer with a puzzled expression and asked him if he could speak English. The Englishman, a little annoyed, repeated his request, adding a few decibels to his utterance for the sake of clarity, but still failing to make himself understood by the owner. At that point I decided to intervene and I volunteered to 'translate' what the young man was trying to say, and the owner finally understood. My 'translation' was not into Lao, but into English. The problem was that the English graduate was using his own local variety of English, popularly known as 'Estuary English', and did not seem to be aware that the glottal stop he was producing in his pronunciation of 'water' as /wɔʔə/ made the word totally incomprehensible to the owner of the food stall, thus causing the only instance of communication breakdown of that evening.

Anecdote 2

One day, as I was waiting at a bus stop in the campus of Universiti Kebangsaan Malaysia, I had a short conversation with an undergraduate student from China. I enquired about how he liked Malaysia, and he replied that he felt comfortable, that people were friendly, the weather always warm and the food tasty. The only negative comment to make, he said, was about the English language. I asked him to elaborate, and he said that he did not like the way Malaysians spoke English. I wanted more clarification: did he find it difficult to understand when people spoke to him? He stated he had no problem in that regard. Did people struggle to understand his English? Again, that was not the case. Still, he was not satisfied with Malaysians' English and he would have preferred to study somewhere where 'official' English was spoken. That place, he explained, was Britain, even though he had never been there and had never spoken to a British person in his life. The fact that he felt linguistically as comfortable as in other aspects of his experience in Malaysia was not important in his judgement. Indeed, in his perception that may well have been a confirmation of Malaysians' sub-standard level of English: since he was convinced that his own English was imperfect, the fact that it seemed to be perfectly adequate in Malaysia must have meant that the people he was interacting with were using equally imperfect English. The place where perfect English was spoken, its real home, was somewhere else, far and unknown.

Anecdote 3

My friend John, an Englishman, was the protagonist in a telling incident while he was spending a few days in France. He went into a shop to buy something and, as he doesn't speak French, he addressed the shopkeeper in English. It was obvious that the shopkeeper was not very pleased and she answered in French and so, in the absence of a common language, the transaction proceeded with some difficulty and coldness. A couple of days later John had to go back to the same shop. He was with his Russian wife this time and they were speaking Russian. He turned to the shopkeeper and, forgetting for a moment what language he was speaking, addressed the woman in Russian. The shopkeeper immediately asked if he could speak English and so John said, "Da, I can speak English." This time the transaction was friendly and went very smoothly.

These three anecdotes represent three different perceptions of the English language. The first incident is open to interpretations. Some might take it as evidence of the fact that language standards among the English youth is falling rapidly and, in support of their conviction, would probably cite linguistic 'aberrations' such as those heard at bar counters ("anifink else?") or read in university undergraduates' essays ("I would of thought…"). Others might object that many of these are features of a form of English that contributes to group identity and that similar phenomena of what is mistakenly taken to be linguistic deterioration have always occurred in all languages. Others still might see this incident as indicative of native speakers' poor ability to make themselves understood in international encounters, as is also shown by the prompt wearing of the interpreter's headphones by English-knowing delegates at European Parliament meetings when some British MEPs are about to speak.

I share the latter interpretation. Some linguists (e.g. Deterding and Kirkpatrick, 2006) identify the stress-based rhythm typical of British English as a culprit for its relatively lower intelligibility in international communication. While I agree with this hypothesis, I also think that the matter is also one of attitude, in the sense that some British speakers of English see themselves as the rightful owners of the language by virtue of a 'genetic' connection to it. Consequently, they are less willing to accommodate their way of speaking in order to facilitate comprehension and, according to this perception, problems of intelligibility can only be due to the interlocutor's imperfect command of the language or failure to hear correctly. In the case of the first anecdote, it was clear that this was indeed the case.

Yet, the aspiration to 'native-like' proficiency remains high in the priorities of many learners, who see the same 'genetic' connection between English, the English and England. This is entirely understandable. The idea that 'official' English is only spoken in England is an obvious one in the mind of someone who would like to approximate linguistic perfection. This aspiration is wholly legitimate and it does not matter if it is based on the following myths:

- that one variety of a language may be qualitatively better than other varieties;
- that the best variety of a language is the oldest or original one;
- that each language or variety has its origin in a country which bears the same name;
- that only the inhabitants of that country are the ones who speak that language or variety correctly.

Fundamentally, all these myths derive from a notion of language as object, which is then qualified with an assortment of attributes, such as good, bad, local, original, new, official, British, Malaysian and so on. As an object, a language is also something that can be owned, accepted and refused. The genetic connection between a language and a particular country and its people also causes sentiments of admiration or resentment.

In the third anecdote, clearly the shopkeeper had nothing against the English language *per se*. Perhaps she was not too fond of English people, but that is a stereotypical assumption that I wish to avoid. I am more inclined to believe that she resented the fact that John was using *his* language in *her* country. When he appeared to be Russian the crucial difference was that English functioned as a lingua franca and its ownership was equally shared between the shopkeeper and the 'Russian' customer. By contrast, in the first encounter the shopkeeper perceived a clear imbalance: language ownership was not equally shared, since for John English was not a lingua franca but his own language. What was more, this language of his had all the power of a world language. The difficulty arose from the shopkeeper's impossibility to reconcile her objectified view of English as a socioculturally located foreign language with its role as a de-nationalised lingua franca.

As English continues to expand and establishes itself as the international lingua franca of choice, as it is increasingly used as a medium of instruction, and as a growing number of children are brought up learning it from a very young age, the question of its *location* becomes more pressing and the main tenet of this book is that possible answers will have to consider its *relocation*.

1
English in the World

1.1 Introduction

The title of this book is purposely ambiguous and invites questions: what is the current *location* of English? Is the relocation of English taking place? If so, where, how and why is it being relocated? This first chapter introduces the main themes of the book and sets in motion a discussion that will consider various aspects of the notion *(re-)location*. In the simplest and most intuitive sense of the word, the location of English could be taken as being England, in the same way as the location of Italian may be Italy and the location of Japanese Japan. This morphological similarity often includes the names of nations and makes the country–nation–language association almost a genealogical one: it seems to be in the natural order of things that Thai is the language of the Thai people and of Thailand, that German is the language of the German people and of Germany and so on. However, the correspondence between language, nation and territory is always a construct (see Chapter 2), and many languages have gone beyond it, their diffusion reaching larger areas than that of a single territory. The language that has done so in the most spectacular way is English, which, in the course of the last four centuries, has stretched well beyond England, to become the world's largest lingua franca.

Accordingly, it is common to hear and read that English is a 'global language' (Crystal, 1997/2003) or a 'world language'. In a purely physical sense, what these expressions mean is that English has some presence in nearly every country in the world. From this point of view, English is unique, in that no other language is currently so widespread. Other international languages such as Arabic and Spanish tend to be spoken in specific geographical areas, while the use of French is in decline in many former French colonies (e.g. in what used to be called Indochina). English, therefore, is the only international language without precise geographical boundaries or clear coordinates. In itself, this constitutes an unprecedented form of relocation of a language out of its original home, at least from a physical point of view. This book takes this as an obvious starting point for a discussion that will embrace other aspects of the notion *relocation*.

1.2   Changing the conceptualisation of English

Despite its enormous proportions, the spread of English in the world has not taken place in the same way and with the same effects everywhere, and the presence of English is very uneven. The adjective 'global', in this sense, may be an exaggeration. There are parts of the world where English is the only language spoken by the majority of people (e.g. rural England), territories where it is an unknown language (e.g. rural China), while in most cases it is part of the linguistic ecology of diverse and multilingual communities (e.g. urban Malaysia). This lack of uniformity makes the task of drawing a map of English in the world very challenging. There is no single method of scrutiny that would produce satisfactory results. Even apparently objective data of the most basic type, namely, to consider whether or not English is an official language, will not even begin to shed any useful light. In the United States, for example, English is not an official language at the federal level, while it has official status in many former British colonies in Africa and Asia.

The status, the forms and the functions of English in the world (from now on, EIW) constitute an area which has attracted a growing amount of interest in the last 40 years, especially since the 1970s. Within this area, there have been two interrelated focal points: (a) the affirmation of English as the language of global currency, and (b) the many varieties of English that emerged as a result of British imperialism. By and large, the study of EIW has been approached from one or both of the two perspectives. Scholars like David Crystal (1997/2003) and David Graddol (1997, 2006), for example, have produced important publications which are general accounts on the history (including hypotheses about the future) and geography of English in the world. Others, like Peter Trudgill and Manfred Görlach, have devoted their attention to the identification and the description of the linguistic features that distinguish the range of varieties of English worldwide (see Trudgill and Hanna, 1982; Görlach, 1991, 1995, 1998, 2002; Trudgill, 2004). These studies are predominantly descriptive in nature and tend to focus on English as a code.

Crucially, however, the object 'English language' is not an isolated entity. As all languages, English is an integral and inalienable part of the lives of the people who use it. This is a fundamental principle in the linguistic theory which sees language as being embedded in its social context (see, among others, Halliday, 1978, 1985/1994; Hodge and Kress, 1988; Halliday and Matthiesen, 2004). It is also a key concept in sociolinguistics, the branch of applied linguistics which most preponderantly underpins work in the area of English in the world. Within this optic, language is intrinsic in most of the tasks we carry out daily, and, in addition, it is fundamental in establishing and maintaining social relations, it contributes to defining the identities of individuals, groups and nations, it can be used to grant or deny access to knowledge and power and it can be a determining factor in one's social status.

A number of scholars, therefore, have worked from a more decidedly social perspective and have explored and discussed not so much the spread of English or its varieties *per se* as their meaningfulness in terms of people's identity, sociopolitical status and power. Robert Phillipson is one of those who have more strongly problematised the expansion of English in the world, condemning its subtle imperialistic drive (1992, 2003, 2008). A social stance has also been adopted in the area of language variation. Among others, Braj Kachru, one of those who initially contributed to shaping this field of study, has concentrated his attention on the pluralisation of English but, again, not so much, or not only, in terms of linguistic features, but also in terms of the roles and functions that different Englishes play, especially in postcolonial settings (Kachru, 1986, 2005). A dominant theme in Kachru's work has been the necessity for all Englishes to be recognised in an egalitarian way.

Hence, a further subdivision within the area of EIW is one between a descriptive and a critical approach. Taking this into account, it is possible to draw a simplified diagram showing how these two approaches intersect with the 'global English' and the 'varieties' approaches mentioned above, thereby revealing four different focal points (Table 1.1), namely,

- the history and the geography of English in the world
- political issues around the spread of English
- formal differences among the different varieties of English
- the plurality and equality of Englishes in the world.

Predictably, the real boundaries between the four sectors are not as clear-cut as the diagram suggests, since conceptualisations of EIW

Table 1.1   Four approaches to the study of English in the world

English in the world		
Focus	Descriptive	Critical
English as a global language	History and Geography e.g. D. Crystal	Politics e.g. R. Phillipson
Varieties of English	Dialects e.g. P. Trudgill	Plurality and Equality e.g. B. Kachru

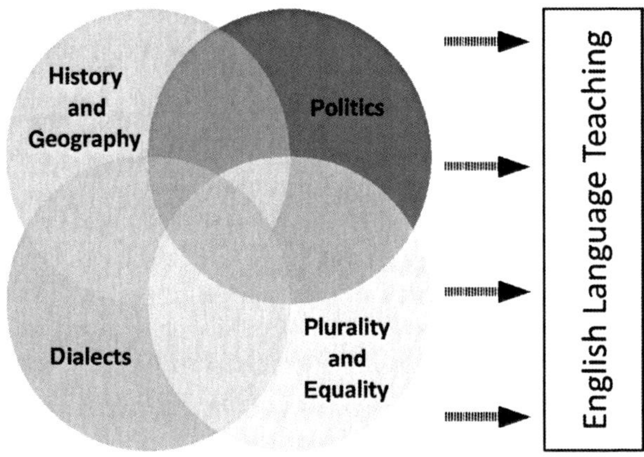

Figure 1.1   An enhanced version of the four-approach model

can be both descriptive and critical and/or may focus on the international dimension of English as well as on local ones. Furthermore, such conceptualisations often underpin pedagogical concerns and this preoccupation is therefore an additional layer to be added to the model. Figure 1.1 is an enhanced and more complete version of the four-approach model, taking into account both the possibility of overlaps among the approaches and the projection towards English language teaching (ELT).

1.3   A paradigm shift

Based on the fact that English has relocated and set roots in so many different parts of the world, much of the literature produced in this broad academic field has emphasised the necessity of a paradigm shift in the conceptualisation of English. Generally, there has been insistence on the urgency to decentralise our view of the English language and adopt a more egalitarian and democratic perspective. This type of concern, which began to be expressed in the mid-1960s, made ground in applied linguistics towards the mid-Eighties, when Randolph Quirk and Braj Kachru, representing respectively conservative and progressive stances, engaged in a debate over the desirability of promoting one monochrome (British) standard English versus recognising the validity and suitability of different varieties of English in different parts of the world.

Indeed, as Chapter 3 recounts in more detail, the whole field was, and to some extent still is, characterised by debate centred upon the relocation of English. The academic area that came to be known as 'World Englishes' (WE) had as its main interest the emergence and development of varieties of English in postcolonial contexts and argued strongly for their full recognition on a par with British and American Englishes. Later, the research field that, towards the end of the millennium, developed virtually as a spin-off of WE began to enlarge the scope of interest by focussing its attention beyond postcolonial settings, namely, on contexts where English is primarily used as a foreign language and as a lingua franca. Researchers working in this area call it ELF, an acronym of English as a lingua franca (see Chapter 5). In strong opposition of conservative and purist positions, the decentralising agenda of both WE and ELF posits that the ownership of the language is not (at all) the prerogative of the native speakers, and that non-native forms of English are as valid as the varieties found in the birthplace of the language. The paradigm shift that has been advocated can be synthesised as shown in Table 1.2:

Table 1.2   The paradigm shift in the conceptualisation of English

From	To
English as the language of Britain	English as the language of many other countries
Emphasis on English as a native language	Emphasis on English as a second language or as a lingua franca
English as a possession of 'native speakers'	English as owned by whoever uses it
English best spoken and best taught by 'native speakers'	Language proficiency and ability to teach not the same; bilingual teachers preferable
One monochrome standard of English	Many equally valid varieties of English
English as the vehicle of Anglosaxon culture	English as capable of expressing any culture

1.4   The location of this book

This broad academic area has been characterised by vibrant activity, especially in the last two decades, and continues to expand and produce research and publications whose contribution to the understanding of EIW is of great significance. This book aligns itself particularly decidedly with the general principles of the decentralising agenda that forms such a fundamental element in this area of study. However, an important postulate underpinning the central idea of the book is that this dynamic activity has tended to be rather inward-looking, in the sense that the paradigm shift outlined in Table 1.2 has not really taken place in a tangible way outside of academia. In particular, while pedagogical concerns constitute a very important area of interest in EIW research, the trajectory from research and academic enquiry to the real world of ELT has not progressed much beyond the level of theory and has therefore not completed its course. As Jennifer Jenkins noted a few years ago,

> ... while this paradigm shift is finally gaining acceptance in theory, in practice it has so far had little impact on applied linguistic research design and even less on English language teaching or teaching materials.
>
> (Jenkins, 2002, p. 83)

The question is that there seems to be "a problematic lack of connection between world Englishes research and the teaching of English as a foreign language" (Matsuda, 2002, p. 420), probably due to the fact that "adequate attention has not been given to a pedagogic area that matters most: classroom methodology" (Kumaravadivelu, 2003, p. 540). Academia may therefore be guilty of being too parochial in its reluctance to extend its gaze beyond its own confines: "Far too often, we publish for the attention of our colleagues and to advance knowledge but do not care much about the fate of English in schools" (Bamgboṣe, 2001, p. 361). Rather more drastic is the claim that "seldom have so many talented men and women worked so long and so hard and achieved so little" (Dasgupta, 1993, p. 137). This quotation has been cited by Alastair Pennycook (2003, p. 521), one of the acutest critic of established canons within the EIW field.

Indeed, perhaps the best piece of evidence of the fact that the paradigm shift in Table 1.2 has not really materialised can be found in one of the latest papers by Braj Kachru, the scholar who probably more insistently, and for longer, than anybody else has advocated its necessity. Here, Kachru (2009) reiterates all the main points, the issues and the challenges that he has been discussing for over 30 years. First of all, the recognition of the validity of varieties of English other than the perceived standard has not taken place. While English has diversified and has "ceased to be exclusively Eurocentric, Judeo-Christian and Western [...] it is not that other Asian and African canons are necessarily accepted or recognized – far from that" (2009, p. 176). Indeed,

> The opening up of the language, and the multiculturalism in the language, does not mean that these multi-strands [...] have been accepted by the linguistic vigilantes or the power elite. That has yet to happen.
>
> (2009, p. 177)

Kachru's definitive admission that the paradigm shift is still in the future could not be clearer: "our current paradigms of constructs and teaching of English continue to be based on monolingual and monocultural – and essentially Western – traditions of creativity and canon formation" (2009, p. 180). Two interrelated aspects seem to have remained relatively unaffected: (a) the preference for British English and American English as models for teaching and learning, and (b) the assumed superiority of the 'native speaker' as the ideal user and teacher of English. Efforts to decentralise the notion *English language* have therefore been not as successful as one would have hoped. The first part of the book takes a critical look at two of the main articulations of the four-approach model, the WE and, more recently, the ELF frameworks, and argues that their conceptualisations of EIW have been thwarted by some important contradictions and may have also produced results antithetic to the purported aims.

In particular:

- emphasis on categorisations and distinctions has contributed to setting strong demarcation lines between varieties and users of English; and
- in turn, the focus on difference has implicitly supported the idea that some Englishes may be more traditional, original and pure than others, and that the speakers of such Englishes may therefore represent models to emulate – the polar opposite of what the best part of EIW academic activity aims to achieve.

Thus, an important aim of this book is to construct a critique, at times sharp, of some of the discoursal practices and conceptualisations that characterise this area of academic enquiry. However, I would like to clarify that such critique is borne out of utmost respect, esteem and appreciation for the work of colleagues who have spent entire careers developing an academic area to which I hope this book can make a small contribution. I share the same aims and I believe that scholars and researchers interested in studying and understanding EIW are faced with considerable conceptual challenges and it is primarily for this reason that different opinions emerge as to how those aims can best be achieved.

1.5 The categorisations of English

One of the biggest challenges in this academic field has been the overwhelming size of EIW and, especially, the lack of uniformity in all its aspects. Consequently, one of the primary objectives has been that of developing schematic models that would help grasp and describe EIW in cognitively manageable ways. A preponderant strategy to deal with variation and differences has been to regularise and encapsulate them into categories that could be more readily understood. Thus, the roles and the forms of English, as well as the geographical and historical dimensions of its spread, have all been segmented and classified. Table 1.3 shows the categorisations that are most common in the relevant literature.

Table 1.3 The categorisations of English in the world

Users of English	Roles of English	History and geography	Varieties of English
Native speakers	Native language	Inner Circle	British English, American English, Australian English, etc.
Non-native speakers	Second language	Outer Circle	Singaporean English, Indian English, Nigerian English, etc.
	Foreign language Lingua franca	Expanding Circle	Chinese English, Japanese English, Thai English, etc.

Although the validity and effectiveness of such categorisations have been questioned by various scholars in the field, most of the terminology that defines them still enjoys common currency. This is partly because of the lack of established better alternatives. The problem, however, is that the use of such terminology entails, or strongly suggests, either agreement with, or at least tacit acceptance of, the distinctions it names. This creates paradoxical situations where certain terms may be used by the same scholars who otherwise express antipathy for them. The distinction between 'native speakers' (NS) and 'non-native speakers' (NNS), for example, has been criticised repeatedly and with particular vigour and has been considered a flawed and misleading dichotomy (see, among many others, Rampton, 1990; Davies, 1991, 2003, 2004; Rajagopalan, 1997; Brutt-Griffler and Samimy, 2001). Still, the terminological distinction between NS and NNS users of English is routinely referred to in order to demonstrate various aspects of the linguistic behaviours of the two groups, including the lack of difference between them.

One of the main arguments that I wish to posit in this book is that such categories are not only inaccurate and outdated, but they are also decidedly harmful, as they contribute to erecting psychological and ideological barriers among users of English as well as between them and the English language. It is precisely on this point that the paradox becomes even more apparent. Much of the literature about EIW is driven by a strong egalitarian impetus. From Halliday et al. (1964), passing through virtually all publications by Braj Kachru and other scholars in the field, including those produced in the more recent ELF research area, there has been uninterrupted attention to the issue of the equality of varieties and users of English. Yet, such equality has been posited largely on the basis of distinctions, and, what is more, on distinctions whose validity has repeatedly been put into question. As long ago as 1982, Ferguson recommended the following:

> The whole mystique of the native speaker and the mother tongue should be quietly dropped from the linguist's set of professional myths about language.
>
> (1982, p. vii)

Nearly 30 years later, the native speaker and other myths are still held on to tenaciously. Attempts to drop them have been rather tepid and have not gone much further than the use of scare quotes. In this book I suggest that not only should the NS/NNS distinction be dropped, but so should also *all* the other categorisations in Table 1.3, as they are divisive, encourage constructs of inequality and are, therefore, ultimately misleading (see Chapter 4).

1.6 Measuring English

Despite their very dubious validity, the categorisations of EIW are often corroborated by statistical data indicating, with varying levels of precision, the number of speakers in each category. The problem is that such statistics are based on estimates whose accuracy is factually impossible to verify. That is because, first of all, it is extremely hard to establish exactly what characteristics someone's linguistic behaviour should have in order for that person to qualify as a 'speaker of English'. Yes/no labels are not easily applicable here. In some of the European nation-states monolingualism may be the norm, but the planet's linguistic ecology is characterised by hybridity, whereby most people belong to bi- or multilingual communities, where different languages are used in different domains, for different reasons and with different levels of proficiency. Moreover, due to constant co-existence and contact, languages intermix as a matter of routine. Code-switching and code-mixing are integral to most people's linguistic *modus operandi*. English, when it is present, is often part of the mix. Attempting to estimate how much of it there is would be like trying to guess the dosage of sugar in a fruit cake after it has been baked.

Yet, one such piece of statistical information is recently being cited with increasing regularity and varying degrees of confidence in conjunction with the native/non-native distinction: that "non-native speakers have come to outnumber native speakers" (Dewey, 2007, p. 332) "by a ratio of more than 2 to 1" (Savignon, 2003, p. 58) or 3 to 1 (Crystal, 2003, p. 69), that "fewer interactions now involve a native speaker" (Graddol, 2006, p. 87) or even that "transactions and interactions in English among non-native speakers (with no native speaker involved) may well outnumber those that involve native speakers interacting with other native speakers" (Taylor, 1995, p. 454). This is often taken as incontestable hard evidence of the fact that the destiny of the language is now wholly in the hands of the larger ranks of so-called non-native speakers. As Graddol (1997) prophetised, "it will be non-native speakers who decide whether a US model, a British one, or one based on a second-language variety will be taught, learned and used" (p. 56) and "second-language and foreign-language speakers [...] will in practice determine the future of global English" (p. 60). This idea is also significantly expanded to include the notion of language 'ownership': "[n]ative speakers may feel the language 'belongs' to them, but it will be those who speak English as a second or foreign language who will determine its world future" (p. 5).

To state that those who considered themselves the proprietors of English may have lost their exclusive rights on the language and need to revise their convictions could be interpreted as the expression of an open-minded, pluralistic and liberal attitude. These may be laudable sentiments, but are not entirely convincing if they are based on flawed categorisations and precarious statistics. But there are other issues to consider. The next section problematises further the notion *ownership of English* as is often discussed in EIW academic discourse.

1.7   The 'ownership of English' discourse

Perhaps the best known and most widely quoted passage in this regard is from a paper by Henry Widdowson entitled "The ownership of English":

> How English develops in the world is no business whatever of native speakers in England, or the United States, or anywhere else. They have no say in the matter, no right to intervene or pass judgement. They are irrelevant. The very fact that English is an international language means that no nation can have custody over it. To grant such custody of the language is necessarily to arrest its development and so undermine its international status. It is a matter of considerable pride and satisfaction for native speakers of English that their language is the international means of communication. But the point is that it is only international to the extent that it is not their language. It is not a possession which they lease out to others, while still retaining the freehold. Other people actually own it.
>
> (Widdowson, 1994, p. 385)

This passage is frequently quoted by those who share a similar belief. However, if Henry Widdowson says that 'native speakers' are irrelevant because English is an international language, I find that seemingly radical statement interesting but, at the same time, also one that is not particularly persuasive. Randolph Quirk, a believer in the use and diffusion of one standard English, once said that "[d]isdain of élitism is a comfortable exercise for those who are themselves securely among the élite" (1985, p. 6). Paraphrasing Quirk's aphorism, one could say that to proclaim that 'non-native speakers' are the sole owners of English is a comfortable exercise for those who are securely among the 'native speakers'.

To presume and to say that the reins of the English language have changed hands from one group of speakers to another merely because of the supposedly higher number of the latter is a little simplistic or perhaps disingenuous. The 'ownership' of a language is a notion that cannot in any way rest upon the size or the international spread of that language. Even assuming that it is a valid concept at all, surely it is up to the individual speaker to feel, or not, a sense of ownership towards it. The feeling of 'ownership' of English can be complex and multifaceted. There can be, for example, a profound ambiguity in the way in which English may be a person's dominant language and yet not fully recognised by that person as their own language. For various reasons, the perception that English is somebody else's language can be deep-rooted. In what seems to be a deictic impossibility, there is sometimes a sense that even though English may be physically located *here*, it really belongs *there*.

It is, crucially, a matter of agency. Regarding a language as one's own, or deliberately refusing to do so, depends on factors that have nothing to do with someone else's vague awareness that one belongs to an imagined community of billions of other speakers of the same language. If those who consider themselves 'native speakers' are not the custodians of English, neither should they be the ones who decide and declare who owns it and who does not. Otherwise, there would be very little substantial difference between leasing it out and giving it away for free, as the agency of the act would remain firmly in the donors' hands, no matter how magnanimous the act may be.

1.7.1   The syntax of agency

In a more recent paper, Seidlhofer and Widdowson stated that

> Although it is acknowledged that English is now being appropriated as a lingua franca by users all over the world, and being put to effective communicative without needing to conform to native speaker norms of 'correctness', there remains an entrenched reluctance to grant the same kind of legitimacy to this 'Expanding Circle' variation that is now generally accorded to 'Outer Circle' varieties.
>
> (2009, p. 26)

This passage is emblematic of a type of discourse that confers on academia the role of arbiter of people's linguistic behaviour, even though this self-proclamation is partially concealed by the syntactic lack of a human agent. In "it is acknowledged", who is it that acknowledges? And on what basis? Another significant passive construction is used in saying that legitimacy is now apparently generally accorded to Outer-Circle varieties. Who has the privilege to grant legitimacy to this or that variety of English? Given that there is in fact very little agreement among the actual *speakers* of English in the Outer Circle about the validity of their English, the one described by Seidlhofer and Widdowson seems to be a one-way discoursal process, in which it is linguists who decide what is legitimate and what is not, on behalf of the users of English, who do not have much of a say about their willingness or interest in appropriating the language. The following longer passage is a good example of this type of discourse, where linguists are portrayed as controllers and censors of the language:

The naive notion of a monolithic, uniform, unadaptable, linguistic medium owned by its original speakers and forever linked to their rule(s) has been recognized as simply contrary to the facts, and has therefore given way to the realization that indigenized varieties of English are legitimate Englishes in their own right, accordingly emancipating themselves vis-à-vis British and American standard English. [...]. Outer Circle linguistic independence has, on the whole, been given the linguistic seal of approval.

[...]. [P]rofessional linguists have so far shown only limited interest in describing 'lingua franca' English as a legitimate language variety. [...]. So, while the Outer Circle has at long last successfully asserted its right to appropriate the language for the expression of its diverse cultures and identities, while postcolonial literatures flourish and language use by writers such as Achebe, Okara, Rushdie, Saro-Wiwa and many others constitutes a prolific area of research, Expanding Circle English is not deemed worthy of such attention: users of English who have learned the language as a foreign language are expected to conform to Inner Circle norms, even if using English constitutes an important part of their lived experience and personal identity. No right to 'rotten English' for them, then.

(Seidlhofer and Jenkins, 2003, p. 142)

The syntactic pattern that emerges here is characterised by (a) passive constructions with 'professional linguists' as the agent and (b) clauses with a non-human agent:

Passive constructions with 'professional linguists' as agent

Subject	Predicate
Idea of monolithic English	Recognised as naïve
Outer-Circle independence	Been given seal of approval
Expanding-Circle English	Not deemed worthy of attention
Expanding-Circle users of English	Expected to conform to Inner-Circle norms

Clauses with a non-human agent

Subject	Predicate
Indigenised varieties of English	Emancipating themselves
The Outer Circle	Asserted right to appropriate English
Postcolonial literatures	Flourish
Postcolonial writers' language	Constitutes prolific area of research
Using English	Constitutes important part in …

A human agent appears in a relative clause while the only main clause with an active construction and a human agent has 'professional linguists' as agent. Linguists are therefore depicted as being very much in control of the situation. They are the ones who have recognised the naïvety of the monolithic notion of English and the legitimacy of Outer-Circle varieties of English and have given their 'seal of approval' to the 'independence' to those varieties, which have consequently emancipated themselves. The Outer Circle has thus been empowered to assert the right to appropriate English and mould it to suit its own needs, while users of English in the Expanding Circle have not yet been given the same right to 'rotten English' and are still expected to follow the norms of the Inner Circle.

It may seem that I am quibbling about syntax here, but form is inalienable from content and there are fundamental questions of content to consider. First of all, the ways in which postcolonial societies position themselves towards the languages of their former masters is not something that can be decided by linguists' expressions of democratic and egalitarian sentiments. The ownership and the appropriation of

English, as well as the right to subvert its rules, have very little to do with what linguists have to say about them. They reside intimately within the conscience, individual and/or collective, of speakers of English. Those who do feel a sense of ownership towards the language do not require authorisation from professional linguists, whose seals of approval are of little consequence.

1.7.2   Academic discourse and public discourse

Secondly, the problem with this kind of academic discourse is that it offers a distorted representation of reality outside its own confines. While it may be true that applied linguists generally agree that all language varieties are of equal standing in terms of their intrinsic linguistic value, to say that the Outer Circle has asserted the right of ownership of English misleadingly projects that egalitarian idea onto a wider discourse that is only an imagined one. Joseph (2004) makes a valid point when, with reference to Hong Kong, he notes the following:

> Linguists risk having only a very partial understanding of the linguistic situation if we dismiss the popular perception outright because it is contradicted by our 'scientific' data. We would do better to think in terms of 'stories': linguists have a different story concerning language in Hong Kong than the one that has emerged in public discourse. Both matter in respects so different that it makes little sense to compare them; but in any case surely the last thing we want to say is that the story in public discourse does not matter. It matters very much indeed. It is through such stories that a society constitutes and maintains itself, determines the direction in which it will develop, and creates an identity and, when necessary, a resistance.
>
> (2004, p. 160)

Linguists often attempt to superimpose their own story about the qualitative equivalence of languages and varieties onto public discourse stories of appropriation, ownership and even subversion in the societies where those languages and varieties are used. This is frequently done, for example, by referring to a selected list of postcolonial creative writers, like Raja Rao and Chinua Achebe, who put the language question at the centre of their concerns and wrote about the ways in which they resolved their dilemmas of using an imperial language by altering it to suit their own cultural environments. These writers' reflections are then amplified and portrayed as evidence of how English has been appropriated and has come to form a healthy part of the linguistic ecology in

Outer-Circle settings. Referring to the Malaysian context, Mandal, for example, observes the following:

> Academics, arts practitioners and other social actors in Malaysia have foregrounded a lively hybrid cultural identity in which English has been localized and effectively made a lingua franca alongside Malay. In this regard, English is no longer the preserve of England [...]. In Malaysia, as in other former British colonies, postcolonial nationals have appropriated the language.
>
> (2000, p. 1012)

However, academics, arts practitioners and the social actors that Mandal refers to represent only a very small minority in any society, a minority whose specialism is precisely the craft of language. In this sense, the use of 'rotten English' is not so much a right as a privilege of those whose social, linguistic and historical awareness allow them to bend language to their purposes, as does the protagonist of John Agard's poem 'Listen Mr Oxford don':

> I slashing suffix in self-defence
> I bashing future wit present tense
> and if necessary
> I making de Queen's English accessory / to my offence

Ken Saro-Wiwa's use of 'rotten English' in one of his novels was "a deliberate choice intended to depict character or to reflect the disorderly state of the society in which the novel is based" (Bamgboşe, 1997, p. 12). Whether creative writers' linguistic preoccupations and strategies are shared by the majority of people in the community is not something that can be taken for granted. After all, deviation from norms is in the very essence of literary language. The deliberate and systematic alteration of English is the prerogative of a very restricted group of people, a highly educated elite, and postcolonial settings are no exception. Rather than aimed at forging and codifying a national variety of English, the formal alteration of the English language was perceived as a way of attaining a degree of independence and autonomy. After all, Kamala Das called her distortions of English "mine and mine alone". Many creative writers, everywhere in the world, have used local forms of English in their texts, but those forms cannot be said to necessarily represent national varieties of English (see, among others, Parakrama, 1995). In former British colonies, including Malaysia, English is still very much at the centre of debate and controversy over the status that should be accorded to it. English may have been localised, but in the public discourse there is a great deal of uncertainty and anxiety about that very localisation, as is discussed in Chapter 6.

1.8 Expert vs layman

Sometimes linguists' confidence in the righteousness of their liberal and open-minded convictions acquires clear patronising tones. Mesthrie and Bhatt (2008, pp. 26–27) cite an illuminating episode recounted by David Crystal (2001, p. 61) where a conference participant asked him if his "notion of linguistic tolerance of English extended to such things as the errors foreigners made". Crystal's reply was that "it all depended on what you mean by an error" and proceeded to mention "I am knowing" as an example of normal grammatical structure in the Indian subcontinent. Subsequently, on being asked whether a Frenchman should be corrected if he said "I am knowing", Crystal responded that the correction would not be necessary if the person was learning Indian English. At this point, "[his] interlocutor's face told [him] that the concept of a Frenchman learning Indian English was, at the very best, novel." Then, after a pause, the person asked, "Are you saying that...we should be letting our teachers teach Indian English, and not British English?" To which Crystal's answer was that "[i]f the occasion warranted it, yes." At this point the person said that he did "not like the sound of that" and left in a hurry, apparently "upsetting a glass of wine in the process".

The intention here may well have been to reiterate the point that those that are seen as 'errors' are often, in fact, instances of regional linguistic variation. However, this anecdote is a revealing example of the 'expert vs layman' construct put into practice. Embedded within the main discourse of the dialogue reported above is a discernible subnarrative that tells how the expert, open-minded and forward-looking linguist finds it subtly pleasurable to shock the uninformed TESOL (Teaching English to Speakers of Other Languages) practitioner, clearly portrayed as naïvely entrenched in traditional views about language. Such an opposition is characterised as outlined below:

EXPERT (LINGUIST)	LAYMAN (TESOL PRACTITIONER)
Knowledgeable	Ignorant
Open-minded	Narrow-minded
Forward-looking	Traditionalist
Intelligent	Naïve

Interestingly (or worryingly), the list above can be superimposed, without modification, to the superior/inferior contraposition typical of the coloniser's representations of the colonised (see Pennycook, 1998):

THE COLONISER (SUPERIOR)
Knowledgeable
Open-minded
Forward-looking
Intelligent

THE COLONISED (INFERIOR)
Ignorant
Narrow-minded
Traditionalist
Naïve

The delegate's clumsy departure at the end of the conversation accentuates the element of derision that was directed at him in the story. One can imagine the smile on David Crystal's face as the knocked glass of wine marked his intellectual victory over his opponent. In fact, more seriously, Crystal's interlocutor's abrupt leaving can be seen as emblematic of the difficulty of communication, and the seemingly unbridgeable gap, between the expert and the layman, between learned academia and down-to-earth classroom. The 'expert vs layman' construct describes a binary opposition where the members of the two communities rarely meet.

1.9 A matter of perspective

Another related point that should always be borne in mind is the dangers, or at least the potential problems, inherent in describing and analysing sociolinguistic realities to which one is only an outsider. Canagarajah (1999) is very clear about it:

> A perspective generated from the periphery community by an insider to that community is badly needed in applied linguistic circles today. At a time when multiculturalism and diversity are fashionable movements in the center, knowledge construction in ELT, as in other academic fields, is still dominated by Western scholars. Realities of periphery communities and center influences are often discussed by center scholars, which accounts for some of their limitations (Phillipson, 1992; Holliday, 1994; Pennycook, 1994). The location of these scholars prevents their well-intentioned books from representing adequately the interests and aspirations of periphery communities.
>
> (1999, p. 5)

Canagarajah makes an entirely valid point here, and it is a matter of intellectual honesty to deal with it. The Western domination of academia in applied linguistics and ELT is still an undeniable fact, although I also optimistically think that, a decade later, the situation has improved, if slightly. The appointment, in 2005, of Canagarajah as editor of *TESOL Quarterly*, one of the most important and prestigious journals in the field, was a significant step in the right direction. As for the insider/outsider question, I think it should be viewed from three separate points of view. First, if considered in relation to the issue of Western domination of applied linguistics and the necessity for wider participation with the more prominent inclusion of work by scholars and researchers from 'periphery' countries, and if the 'insider' is a member of a 'periphery' community, it is clear that more insider knowledge is desirable. Second, the insider's perspective will be preferable to the outsider's in situations where scholars from the centre assign to themselves the mission of speaking out for the voiceless periphery, with the inevitable result of sounding unconvincing or even patronising. The third point of view, however, is less categorical. The preference for the insider's perspective or the outsider's depends on what a particular study purports to find out and attain. While outsiders are probably not the most suitable people to discuss the interests and aspirations of communities of which they are not members, they might have an advantage if they aim to articulate more objective and neutral descriptions that sometimes a detached external perspective is more capable of. As an afterword to these reflections, I would also like to add that I do not necessarily see those of 'insider' and of 'outsider' as clear-cut distinct categories. How long does one have to live, work and interact in a community before he/she can successfully claim 'insider' status? Or is birthplace a factor that can preclude this possibility? Equally, when does one begin to lose that status after leaving a community? Or is it part of one's genetic information?

To return to the specific topic of this book, the fundamental point is that information about the opinions, attitudes and perceptions about the English language can only be usefully gathered from the people who hold and, either directly or indirectly, express such opinions, attitudes and perceptions. Canagarajah's ethnographic approach in his own research on students' expressions of resistance to "totalitarian tendencies" (1999, p. 197) is exemplar of the way in which instances of appropriation and ownership can, and should, be sought outside the restricted circles of creative writers.

1.10   A linguistic view of language ownership

The discrepancy between academic discourse and public discourse is thus not insurmountable. Research on language attitudes has a long tradition (see Cavallaro and Ng, 2009, for an overview) and some of it has concentrated specifically on the degree of people's sense of ownership of English in postcolonial settings. In this regard, some researchers have carried out work that considered the extent to which groups of respondents rated the acceptability of certain expressions in their local variety of English. Most notably, Higgins (2003) sought to investigate "the degree to which [outer-circle speakers] project themselves as legitimate speakers with authority over the language" (2003, p. 615). Bokhorst-Heng et al. (2007) and Rubdy et al. (2008) conducted similar studies, in which they aimed to ascertain how Singaporeans "positioned themselves in the process of articulating their orientations to English norms" (2008, p. 40). This research has the clear merit of having obtained data directly from actual speakers in trying to ascertain their sense of language ownership, thereby contributing to filling a research gap as well as a discoursal gap between academia and the general public. In her study, Higgins found that "the speakers from the outer circle displayed less certainty, or lesser degrees of ownership, than did the speakers from the inner circle" (2003, p. 640). Similarly, Bokhorst-Heng et al., whose study focussed on Malay Singaporeans, discovered that their respondents showed "a strong tendency to authenticate their judgements on the basis of exonormative standards" and "felt compelled overall to seek the 'correct' answer and not rely on their own intuition" (2007, p. 442). Interestingly, when the same researchers replicated their own study with Indian Singaporeans, "the informants showed a high degree of ownership of English, as indicated by their ability to make confident judgements and their willingness to rely on their intuitions" (Rubdy et al., 2008, p. 62). This was possibly a reflection of the fact that "a unique feature of the Indian population in Singapore is that this is the only group that extensively uses English as a lingua franca within the community" (p. 42).

1.11   The location of English

These are findings that begin to tell us something more concrete and tangible than do vacuous statements oscillating between the politically correct and the patronisingly pseudo-liberal. I believe that if we are serious about studying such an important concept as the ownership of English, an ethnographic approach is the only possible route. What may well differ, of course, is the individual researcher's own conceptualisation of 'ownership', 'English' and 'language' and, consequently, the methodological details as well as the interpretation of the data. The studies cited above, for example, take a view of ownership that is strictly based on linguistic norms. In my own understanding, by contrast, language ownership goes much further than language as *code*. Indeed, it may well even transcend it. A sense of ownership towards a language can be felt whether or not one feels confident enough about its code as to be able to pass judgements on the correctness of given expressions. It has more to do with how one positions oneself in relation to a language, and what that language represents. Ultimately, the appropriation of English and any subsequent claim of ownership over it constitute a psychological stance and depend on whether one locates the English language within one's own Self or sees it only as a property of the Other.

Chapter 2 explores the relationship between language and 'location' from a historical perspective, namely, in the context of the nineteenth-century European concept of nation-state, when the nexus between language, people and territory began to be forged.

2
Language and Nation Building

Is fearr Gaeilge bhriste, ná Béarla cliste (*Broken Irish is better than clever English*).

—Irish proverb

2.1 Introduction

From a physical point of view, languages can be said to be located in specific territories. This is an idea that became central in the process of nation building in nineteenth-century Europe. It is indeed in that historical and geographical context that, perhaps unwittingly, much of the twentieth-century discourse on language purism and pluralism finds its earliest roots. In the specific case of English, the link with a particular territory probably began to be established earlier. With reference to 1362, when English replaced Norman French as the legislative language of Britain, Seton-Watson observed the following:

> One might [...] risk the generalisation that, though England was a land of human civilisation from the time of Julius Caesar, and even earlier, an English nation and an English language only came into existence in the fourteenth century. From this time only dates the history of England, as opposed to the history of the people of Britain.
> (Seton-Watson, 1977, p. 30)

With these words, Seton-Watson identifies an inextricable link between English and England but, interestingly, it is far from England, and centuries later, that the English language began to be the centre of a discussion in which the role of the language was explicitly connected to that of nation.

2.2 Noah Webster and American English

In the introduction to *A Grammatical Institute of the English Language*, Noah Webster wrote the following:

> Previously to the late war, America preserved the most unshaken attachment to Great-Britain: The kind, the constitution, the laws, the commerce, the fashions, the books, and even the sentiments of Englishmen were implicitly supposed to be the best on earth: not only their virtues and improvements, but their prejudices, and their errors, their vices and their follies were adopted by us with avidity. But by a concurrence of those powerful causes that effect almost instantaneous revolutions in states, the political views of America have suffered total change. She now sees a mixture of profound wisdom and consummate folly in the British constitution; a ridiculous compound of freedom and tyranny in their laws; and a few struggles of patriotism, overpowered by the corruptions of a wicked administration. She views the vices of that nation with abhorrence, their errors with pity, and their follies with contempt.
>
> (Webster, 1783, p. 3)

This statement, which would seem very oddly placed in a modern grammar textbook, is a clear indication that Webster's interests were not just about grammar. From a more specific point of view of language pedagogy, his criticism was directed at British educators, who seemed to derive grammatical norms from Greek and Latin:

> The British writers remark it as one of the follies of their nation, that they have attended more to the study of ancient languages and foreign languages, than to the improvement of their own. [...] This ridiculous practice has found its way into America; and so violent have been the prejudices in support of it, that the whispers of common sense, in favour of our native tongue, have been silenced amidst the clamour of pedantry in favour of Greek and Latin.
>
> (1783, pp. 3–4)

Webster's efforts were not driven solely by his disapproval of what he considered British pedagogical 'follies'. In *Dissertations on the English Language* he made it clear that the codification of American English was inextricably linked to the gained independence of his country from Great Britain:

> As an independent nation, our honor requires us to have a system of our own, in language as well as government. Great Britain, whose children we are, and whose language we speak, should no longer be *our* standard; for the taste of her writers is already corrupted, and her language on the decline. But if it were not so, she is at too great a distance to be our model, and to instruct us in the principles of our own tongue.
>
> (1789, pp. 20–21)

The claim of ownership of an American standard was further reinforced by Webster's confidence that the American and the British versions of English were on irrecoverably divergent paths:

> [...] several circumstances render a future separation of the American tongue from the English, necessary and unavoidable. [...] These causes will produce, in a course of time, a language in North America, as different from the future language of England, as the modern Dutch, Danish and Swedish are from the German, or from one another: Like remote branches of a tree springing from the same stock; or rays of light, shot from the same center, and diverging from each other, in proportion to their distance from the point of separation.
>
> (1789, pp. 22–23)

Webster saw the English language as a British inheritance which was becoming increasingly Americanised. Significantly, the process was unavoidable, given the physical distance between the two countries, but also a *necessary* one. The connection between language and nation was very explicit:

> This language is the inheritance which the Americans have received from their British parents. To cultivate and adorn it, is a task reserved for men who shall understand the connection between language and logic, and form an adequate idea of the influence which a uniformity of speech may have on national attachments.
>
> (1789, p. 18)

Thus, the autonomy of American English was a necessary reflection of the autonomy of the American nation, but it was also very important that the language be kept uniform *within* America. Webster noted how "every State in America and almost every town in each State, has some peculiarities in pronunciation which are equally erroneous and disagreeable to its neighbours" (1783, p. 4) and it was therefore a matter of priority that people would "demolish those odious distinctions of provincial dialects, which are the objects of reciprocal ridicule" (1783, p. 5) and "diffuse an uniformity and purity of *Language*" (1783, p. 11), since "political harmony is [...] concerned in a uniformity of language" (1789, p. 20). Local idiosyncrasies had to be eliminated and a standard form had to be fixed on *"the rules of the language itself,* and the *general practice of the nation"* (1789, p. 27).

Webster's preoccupations were therefore evidently only partly linguistic, as he advocated the necessity for the new American nation to find its own, independent voice. For him it was important that

(a) the differences *between* American English and British English be maximised, in order to highlight the distinctive character of the American nation;
(b) the differences *within* American English be minimised, so that the national variety of English could act as a true force contributing to uniting the nation.

In this way Webster attached great importance to the role of the language in the process of construction of an American national identity. Benedict Anderson, who otherwise tends to downplay the extent to which language has been used politically in the formation of nation-states in the American continent, observes that Webster's efforts represented "a sort of 'European' thinking early at work" (1991, p. 197), and indeed, the link between language and nation building was crucial in European nationalist movements of the nineteenth century.

2.3 Language and nation building in nineteenth-century Europe

When the old dynastic powers based on absolute monarchy and feudalism began to crumble under the pressure of revolutionary movements, the nation-state emerged as a new form of political organisation. Thus, as in these early democracies people were granted more decisional power than they had been in the past, the ability for them to use a common language was deemed of crucial importance. In addition, for nineteenth-century nationalist movements the presence of a common language was essential in the construction of the very idea of 'nation', the existence of which could be demonstrated effectively by the presence of a language which would at the same time unite a group and distinguish them from their neighbours. This was the concept of 'asbau language' theorised by Kloss (1967).

2.3.1   Linguists and codification

Decisions about language were an integral part of the process of nation building. As Wright (2004, pp. 42–68) explains, these concerned the choice of the variety that was to become the official language of the state, the formulation of prescriptive norms that would guarantee the stability and uniformity of the chosen national language as well as its differentiation from other (neighbouring) national languages and policies to ensure that those norms would be taught and learned by the population everywhere across the national territory. In the implementation of national language policies, linguists and literates had an important role to play. In Italy, for example, novelist and poet Alessandro Manzoni had a strong interest in forging an Italian national language. His most famous novel, *I Promessi Sposi* (*The Betrothed*), is renowned both as a literary masterpiece and as a serious attempt to codify a linguistic model that would be at one time refined and comprehensible by the greatest number of people in the emerging state.

The process of codification of national languages often also included their 'purification' from influences that were considered 'foreign'. This was especially true in cases where a territory had been ruled by a neighbouring power. Norway, for example, was under Danish rule for more than four centuries and after independence was gained in 1814, the question of the language became a matter of paramount importance. Philologist Ivar Aasen undertook a meticulous study of Norwegian dialects in order to codify a literary language that would be purely Norwegian and devoid of any Danish influences. This work produced the publication of *Grammar of the Norwegian Dialects* (1848) and *Dictionary of the Norwegian Dialects* (1850), which codified what came to be known as *Nynorsk*, contrasting with the Dano-Norwegian language used by the urban elite.

It is clear that Aasen's efforts were not dissimilar, in spirit, to Webster's and those of other linguists operating in the same historical period and following the same rubric. The normative language descriptions that they produced were aimed at codifying languages with a clear national identity attached to them. It is in this sense that it is possible to affirm that, ultimately, national languages are "almost always semi-artificial constructs" and "the opposite of what nationalist mythology supposes them to be, namely the primordial foundations of national culture and the matrices of the national mind" (Hobsbawm, 1992, p. 54).

2.4   Language and imagined communities

Hobsbawm's use of the word 'mythology' with reference to nationalism is key here, since it highlights its fundamentally constructionist matrix. That is because it was essential for the nation-state to assert its right over a particular territory and 'nation' provided a suitable concept that could be exploited in relation to its connections to an 'original' land of which it was then possible to claim legitimate ownership. Consequently, the concept of nation, defined as 'imagined community' by Anderson (1991), needed to be substantiated with as much 'evidence' as possible:

> Its invention must, in other words, be forgotten. For if invented, the nation might be perceived as merely artificial, arbitrary, contingent in character, thus making its validity very shallow indeed. Instead the myth must be made that the nation is a *natural* entity, with a deep-rooted authenticity that is being rediscovered.
>
> (Joseph, 2004, p. 115)

It is for this reason that genetics and ethnicity have always featured prominently in national narratives. The Nazi propaganda, to cite an extreme form of nationalist narrative, built the myth of the German people as the direct descendants of the Aryans. More moderate versions of similar stories exist about nations all over the world, even in relation to sub-national groups. In Malaysia, society is organised and regulated around the concept of 'race'. The Malays, the dominant group, call themselves *bumiputra*, 'children of the soil', to signal their position as ancestral inhabitants of the Malay Peninsula and justify the constitutional privileges that they enjoy. In Italy, the political party of the *Lega Nord* ('Northern League'), which seeks a greater autonomy and even the complete independence of the wealthy northern regions from the rest of the country, has rapidly created its own national narrative, according to which northern people are the direct descendants of the Celts, and therefore ethnically different from southern Italians, who are of another, Mediterranean stock.

   In modern societies, however, ethnicity is often unconvincing as a narrative device in creating and cementing group identity, and language can thus complement or even replace ethnicity in that role:

> In such biologically complex societies, where the concept of 'racial purity' makes no sense and where intra-group physical variation may be as great or greater than that between groups, group recognition on physical criteria is, despite all racist or nationalist rhetoric, unreliable. Thus a cultural diacritic such as language becomes the salient marker

of group difference and minor variations of dialect and accent which allow members of an exclusive group to recognise each other as such are emphasised.

(Wright, 2000, p. 63)

Within this construct, "language [...] appears a convenient and incontrovertible means of establishing difference; a means which cannot be called into question as can some other cultural artefacts" (McColl Millar, 2005, p. 30). The existence of language X is thus taken as a precondition for the existence of a nation X, which, in turn, is seen as the ultimate justification for that nation's claim of a particular territory, bearing the same name of the language and the nation. The absolute coincidence of names indicates a primordial, natural and, therefore, unquestionable symbiosis of language, nation and territory. It is for this reason, for example, that the *Northern League* party leaders stress with particular insistence the importance of the 'Padan' languages and highlight their differences from standard Italian. These differences are therefore highly symbolic. As John Joseph has pointed out, this type of trivial linguistic divergences may have the same value in distinguishing a nation from another as do other equally superficial differences:

> reliance on differences of a necessarily subtle order [...] endows even the smallest variation with huge cultural significance. The very essence of a nation can come to be seen as residing within some superficially insignificant idiosyncrasy – the retention of a guttural fricative within the phonetic system, the ceremonial wearing of a kilt or serving of a dish that the neighbours find so repugnant as to make a joke of it.

(Joseph, 2004, p. 106)

And it does not matter how small the difference is:

> there is no preset threshold of difference that a distinct 'language' must reach. If the desire for a distinct language to be recognised is strong enough, the most minor differences will be invested with the ideological value needed to fill the bill.

(Joseph, 2004, p. 144)

Thais, for example, will state, without doubt, that they speak a different language from that spoken in Laos, regardless of the fact that people from either side of the river Mekong, tracing the border between the two countries, understand each other well. The use of language difference as a marker of national identities and distinctions is indeed not confined to the past. Europe is currently in a post-nation-state phase, where associations are forged at the super-national level (i.e. the European Union) and group identities are concurrently sought with increasing vigour at the sub-national level (e.g. in Spain, in the Balkans, etc.). Language continues to play a pivotal role. Silesian separatists in western Poland, for example, are trying to have the Silesian language codified and recognised in order to give more credibility to their cause. Interestingly, while traditional forms of codification such as grammars and dictionaries are not always feasible, especially for smaller languages like Silesian whose status is still unclear, more modern forms are emerging. In May 2008 Silesian language activists launched the Silesian edition of Wikipedia, thereby giving the language an official presence on the Internet and, at the same time, bypassing decisions made by the Polish Government.

This latest type of nationalism continues to highlight, possibly with even more clarity, the fact that the identification of different languages plays an essential role in the identification of different nations and the creation of national identities. In conclusion, it can be said that in the last 200 years, the link between language and nation has been characterised by the necessity to:

- identify and emphasise linguistic differences between a language and those in its vicinity
- systematise those differences into grammar books, dictionaries or more modern forms of codification
- purify the language and purge it of any extraneous elements
- minimise internal variation by ensuring that the language is spoken by all members of a nation.

This brief overview provides part of the frame of reference for the discussion and analysis in the following chapters about English in the world.

3
World Englishes

> Joebell smile, because if is one gift he have it is to talk languages,
> not Spanish and French and Italian and such, but he could talk
> English and American and Grenadian and Jamaican; . . .
>
> —Earl Lovelace, 'Joebell and America'

3.1 Introduction

This chapter provides an overview of when and how academic interest developed around EIW during the 1970s and 1980s, when much
of the debate was centred upon the necessity to break away from traditional purist, monolithic and Anglo-centric views of English towards
broader perspectives which would recognise not only the existence but
also the dignity and validity of different varieties of English around the
world, including non-native ones. This movement can be characterised
as revolutionary, especially since it openly opposed what were regarded
as well-established positions. A major role in initiating this academic
discussion was played by Braj Kachru who, with his book *The Alchemy
of English* (1986), laid out the foundations of the World Englishes (WE)
school of thought.

3.2 The beginning of a revolution

Much of the academic work on English in the world has often provoked,
directly contributed to, or indirectly inspired, debate. As a confirmation
of this, the very foundations of what was about to become an important
body of literature in applied linguistics were, in many ways, laid down
in Braj Kachru's persuasive response (1976) to a paper by Clifford Prator,
who had polemically argued against "the idea that it is best, in a country

where English is not spoken natively but is widely used as the medium of instruction, to set up the local variety of English as the ultimate model to be imitated by those learning the language" (1968, p. 459). In a rhetoric bordering linguistic racism, Prator claimed that "second-language varieties" of English were unsuitable as pedagogical models not only because they were merely imperfect imitations of "mother-tongue varieties" but also because their very existence was far from being established. Any variety of English other than the "mother-tongue" ones was "a tongue caught up in a process that tends to transform it swiftly and quite predictably into an utterly dissimilar tongue" (1968, p. 464). The variety of English in India, for example, was only "a certain linguistic phenomenon that is often popularly and impressionistically labeled 'Indian English'" (1968, p. 464).

Prator's assertions were so misguided, inaccurate and removed from serious sociolinguistic grounding that it was all too simple to controvert them, at least academically. Indeed, his arch-conservative views seemed to be not so much the fruit of sound and rational academic work as the expression of anxiety generated by the fear that, in certain quarters, 'Inner Circle' linguists seemed to be inexplicably willing to release control of the English language and deliver it to others all over the world. In Prator's view, this position was heretical and, hence, completely untenable and those culpable of promoting it were primarily British linguists. He found this "British heresy" particularly well expressed by Halliday et al. (1964), who had observed that, in the 1960s, times were changing in ELT, especially as it came to the adoption of a suitable model of the language:

> Where the choice used to be between American (in a few marginal cases) and British English, now it is between American, British, Australian or other regional variants. English is no longer the possession of the British, or even of the British and the Americans, but an international language which increasingly large numbers of people adopt for at least some of their purposes [...] and this one language, English, exists in an increasingly large number of different varieties.
> (Halliday et al., 1964, p. 293)

Nearly half a century ago, this was a remarkably progressive position, especially in its reference to the idea of decentralised possession of English, and it is perhaps not surprising that it provoked worried and ethnocentric responses such as Prator's. Thus, there were at the time two orientations: one, liberal, based on study and research in applied linguistics, working towards ensuring that the practice of ELT would be informed by the principles and the findings of linguistics and promoting a democratic view of English; the other, reactionary, seeking to resist liberal ideas which were seen as undermining the native speaker's control and the ownership of English and, therefore, as unacceptable.

What happened in the decades that followed was interesting. The field of applied linguistics grew much larger. The very scholars to whom Prator had pointed his accusatory finger continued and expanded their work. Halliday, in particular, went on to develop one of the most influential theories of language in the late twentieth century and to become one of the most highly respected linguists of all times. In the meantime, after his response to Prator's paper, Braj Kachru began what could be termed the 'World Englishes' school of thought, which would take further the liberal stance described above and develop it into a complex and comprehensive sociolinguistic model of English in the world, with important pedagogical implications. Prator's prediction, or hope, that "the doctrine will die a natural death" (1968, p. 460) proved to be spectacularly wrong. And so did his claim that non-native varieties of English were inherently destined to disappear into the oblivion of unintelligibility.

3.3 Debating English

Kachru's response to Prator's paper was a preview of what was to come. It was a strong and clear statement against linguistic purism, ethnocentrism and monoculturalism. Such a statement was a necessary one because, Kachru felt, that kind of linguistic chauvinism was not displayed exclusively by Prator, but was "nurtured by several educated native speakers and educators of English" (1976, p. 222). Kachru articulated his position by first exposing the misconceptions (which he called "sins", echoing Prator's use of the word "heresy") in the purist stance, and then, with particular reference to Indian English, by explaining how "third-world varieties" had their own validity as they formed an integral part of the linguistic repertoire in the sociocultural context in which they were used. Towards the end of his paper he made an invitation that was, at the same time, a wish:

The strength of the English language is in presenting the *Americanness* in its American variety, and the *Englishness* in its British variety. Let us, therefore, appreciate and encourage the Third World varieties of English too. The individuality of the Third World varieties, such as the *Indianness* of its Indian variety, is contributing to the linguistic mosaic which the speakers of the English language have created in the English speaking world. The attitude toward these varieties ought to be one of appreciation and understanding…

(Kachru, 1976, p. 236)

Thus, Kachru took on the debate that began in the 1960s and carried it forward into the 1970s, delineating two camps quite clearly: on one side those who sought to preserve (a) the position of British and/or American English as the only acceptable models and the standard of the language, and (b) the position of the 'native speaker' as the exclusive owner of that normative standard to which everybody else had to comply; on the other side those who had a more pluralistic view of English and recognised the existence and the validity of different uses and varieties of the language worldwide.

Among the latter was Larry Smith, who, in the same year, published a paper in which he offered a very open-minded and democratic view of English, pushing further Halliday et al's idea of shared ownership: "English belongs to the world [...]. It is yours (no matter who you are) as much as it is mine (no matter who I am)" (1976, p. 39). Smith was also decidedly in favour of the recognition of different varieties of English. However, while Kachru focussed his attention primarily on the intranational roles of English in postcolonial settings, Smith emphasised the function of English as an international language:

English is an international auxiliary language. [...] English is one of the languages of Japan, Korea, Micronesia, and the Philippines. It is one of the languages of the Republic of China, Thailand and the United States. [...] English is a language of the world. If you accept this argument, then it is time to stop calling it a foreign language or second language. The name should be EIAL (English as an International Auxiliary Language) which more accurately reflects the present state of English language usage around the globe.

(Smith, 1976, p. 39)

Smith's emphasis on the international role of English meant that his pluralistic position also kept a firm grip on the fundamental singularity of the language:

It is important to note that there is a *single* English language but many varieties. The language of the United States is American English.

> Certainly speakers of American English are identifiable by their pro-
> nunciation, intonation, stress, rhythm, and some vocabulary items
> but the language (the general orthography, lexicology, semantics,
> syntax – the grammar, if you will), is English. It is the same English
> that is spoken in Singapore, however; Singapore English speakers are
> also identifiable by their pronunciation, intonation, stress, rhythm,
> and some vocabulary items.
>
> (Smith, 1976, p. 38, my emphasis)

Consequently, international auxiliary English would have both "the 'flavour' of each country using it" and "an international character" to guarantee intelligibility (Smith, 1976, p. 41).

Although the works cited so far pre-date what was about to become a full-fledged field of study, in retrospect it is possible to clearly identify in them the ancestry of some important positions that would subsequently mark future developments and, often, debate in the conceptualisations of English in the world. These can be outlined as follows:

- the development of the notion of English as an international language, owned by whoever uses it, and characterised by a sufficient
  degree of internal consistency to ensure international intelligibility
  despite instances of local variation;
- the idea that an excessively democratic and tolerant attitude towards
  'non-native varieties of English', whose acceptability and even existence are rather dubious, is counter-productive for the teaching and
  learning of English as a foreign language;
- the necessity for a systematic analysis of the forms and functions of
  English in postcolonial settings, in order to demonstrate not only
  the existence but also the validity of varieties of English other than
  those traditionally seen as representing the standard, namely, British
  English and American English.

A decade later, EIW had become a more established area of academic interest. In 1985 Randolph Quirk and Henry Widdowson edited the pro-ceedings of an international conference held in London the year before and gave the volume the title *English in the World*. Two contributors to the book, Quirk himself and Braj Kachru, continued and developed the debate that had begun 20 years earlier. In his paper, Quirk expressed concern about the fact that it seemed to have become fashionable for linguists to consider all varieties of English equally good and correct and, consequently, to dismiss the notion of standard as unhelpful. He felt that such an attitude was educationally unjustifiable particularly in contexts where English was used as a second or foreign language, since "the relatively narrow range of purposes for which the non-native needs to use English (even in ESL countries) is arguably well catered for by a single monochrome standard form that looks as good on paper as it sounds in speech" (1985, p. 6). Although the tone of Quirk's paper was very distant from Prator's invectives, the essence of its content was not too dissimilar. Indeed, it was almost as if Quirk had reformulated Prator's predicament into a more rational and seemingly logical argument: as English is a world language, used for international communication, it makes sense that it be as uniform as possible and variation kept to an absolute minimum so as not to hinder its communicative function.

Kachru's paper offered a profoundly different perspective. Even if it was not a direct response to Quirk's in form, it was very much so in content. By this time Kachru had developed the ideas that he had been expounding in the previous years and had elaborated a model of English in the world which was to become one of the most influential and best-known descriptions of the uses and users of the language worldwide. The main idea was that there were significant differences in the ways English spread, was acquired and functioned in different parts of the world. Based on those parameters, Kachru identified three categories (Kachru, 1985, pp. 12–14):

- the "Inner Circle", where English was the first language for the majority of people either because the territory was its older historical base (the United Kingdom) or because it had replaced local languages as a result of the annihilation of indigenous populations in certain territories of the former British Empire (e.g. the United States, Australia, etc.);
- the "Outer Circle", where English was an additional language co-existing with other local languages and used intranationally in various domains in postcolonial settings where indigenous people had not been exterminated on a large scale (e.g. India, Nigeria, Malaysia, etc.);
- the "Expanding Circle", where English did not have a historical presence but was growing in importance as the foreign language of choice (e.g. Japan, China, Germany and virtually everywhere else in the world).

This classification was the basis of what came to be known as the Three Circles of English, the most influential model describing the uses and the users of English in the world. Kachru also made a corollary categorisation of varieties of English (1985, pp. 16–17): norm-providing varieties, usually regarded as ideal models of the language, in the Inner Circle; norm-developing varieties, in the process of establishing their own norms but still to some extent looking up to Inner-Circle varieties, in the Outer Circle; and norm-dependent varieties, which relied completely on Inner-Circle models, in the Expanding Circle.

These distinctions were important in showing that a single monochrome form of English could not possibly cater for the range of different users and functions of the language. What Kachru sought to demonstrate was that the plurality of Englishes was not a matter of opinion, but a fact based on complex sociolinguistic realities. Consequently, he also endeavoured to show that more empirical research was required in order not only to describe linguistic differences among varieties of English but also and primarily to understand better the communicative, educational, cultural and creative roles of such varieties. An additional element of enquiry focussed on the attitudes held towards those varieties of English by people who spoke them as well as people who did not.

Kachru's research-based stance made conservative and purist preoccupations appear to be driven by preconceived and quite evidently inaccurate assumptions about the sociolinguistic panorama of English in the world. Quirk's belief that the non-native speaker only used English for "a narrow range of purposes" echoed quite faithfully Prator's supposition that second-language varieties were "reserved for use with specific individuals in a narrowly restricted range of situations" (1968, p. 463). Set against the starkly different and far more variegated sociolinguistic landscape that they aimed to describe, such statements appeared somewhat bizarre. Quite paradoxically, moreover, Quirk's comment on the non-native speaker's supposedly restricted range of purposes for using English co-existed with a description, only a few pages earlier in the same paper, of ESL countries as settings "where English is in widespread use for what we may broadly call 'internal' purposes as well: in administration, in broadcasting, in education" (1985, p. 2). A possible explanation for that self-contradicting epistemological contrast between conjecture and reality is that the contention between those who championed the acceptability of a single English and those who recognised the validity of a plurality of Englishes concerned more than just language varieties.

It will be useful, once again, to take another look at Prator's paper. In describing "the doctrine of establishing local models for TESL", Prator had observed that "such proposals seem to arise spontaneously and inevitably in every formerly colonial area where English has been the principal medium of instruction long enough for the people to begin to feel somewhat *possessive* about the language" (1968, p. 460, my emphasis). As was seen above, Prator unashamedly regarded the "doctrine" as heretical. And it does not seem unreasonable to assume that what he found particularly heretical was that some people began to feel possessive about a language, *his* language, without having the right to do so. It was a matter of genealogy: "The British, American, and other mother-tongue types of English are each the unique linguistic component of the culture that produced them and are inseparable from the rest of that culture. [...] They have sprung from a common linguistic stock [...]" (1968, p. 463). Prator seemed to attach a sacred value to the ancestral roots of English and to the cultural uniformity of their immediate offspring, thereby reiterating the language/people/territory relationship of the nation-state narrative (see Chapter 2) and disregarding even the most obvious forms of cultural diversity characterising his own country. Indeed, his views were in stark contrast with what had taken place in the previous 400 years of North American history, marked by extremely important instances of acculturation of English, that is, the appropriation of the English code by different cultural groups (a phenomenon that Kachru described extensively with reference to the Outer Circle). What Prator meant by "mother-tongue varieties" was actually only a subset of such varieties, namely, those which exhibited more faithfully their Anglosaxon roots. In doing so, he erected very strong boundaries along what he saw as the genetic lineage of the English language. The logical conclusion of the argument was that only those who belonged to that genetic lineage had the right to claim ownership of the English language. Evidently, Prator's views about English were inherently ideological and nearly racist and were, therefore, only marginally concerned with language form. It is in this sense that it is possible to explain the discontinuity between Prator's observations and the sociolinguistic reality that Kachru endeavoured to describe.

To return to Quirk, his position was, as noted earlier, not fundamentally dissimilar from Prator's, even if it lacked the American's racist undertones. His insistence on the necessity for non-native speakers of English to adopt the same standard and to refrain from the fashionable but intrinsically dangerous temptation to regard all varieties as equally valid reflected a view of English which was Anglo-centric and essentially contradictory. On the one hand, he recognised and accepted variation between British and American English, but, on the other hand, he advocated that for everybody else a "single monochrome standard form" (1985, p. 6) should be the model of choice, even in ESL countries, where English was "in widespread use for what we may broadly call 'internal' purposes" (1985, p. 2). Again, there seemed to be a common theme underpinning Prator's and Quirk's stance: the 'non-native speaker' was not in a position to have any degree of agency over the English language, let alone of ownership.

A few years later, Braj Kachru's response to another paper by Randolph Quirk had more explicit traits of a debate. Both papers were published in the journal *English Today*, Quirk's in 1990 and Kachru's in 1991. Quirk was growing increasingly radical: deeply entrenched in defence of the superiority of standard English (a term which could be understood as synonymous to 'British English' through a critical reading of his work) and decidedly distrustful of the quality and the validity of the English used in what he called, unequivocally and rather paradoxically, "non-English-speaking countries" (1990, p. 7). He categorically rejected the idea that institutionalised varieties of English existed in countries outside the Inner Circle and presented such denial not as originating exclusively from his own speculations but as a conviction shared by people in those very countries. He contended that the argument that there should be an Indian English, a Nigerian English, a Ghanian English and so on alongside American and British English would be tenable only "provided there was agreement within each such country that it was *true*, or even that there was a determined policy to *make* it true" (1990, p. 8). However, this did not appear to him to be the case:

> So far as I can see, neither of the conditions obtains, and most of those with authority in education and the media in these countries tend to protest that the so-called national variety of English is an attempt to justify inability to acquire what they persist in seeing as 'real' English.
>
> (1990, p. 8)

According to Quirk, arguing for the existence of valid postcolonial varieties of English was not only linguistically unsound but also pedagogically dangerous:

> No one should underestimate the problem of teaching English in such countries as India and Nigeria, where the English of the teachers themselves inevitably bears the stamp of locally acquired deviation from the standard language ("You are knowing my father, isn't it?").

The temptation is great to accept the situation and even to justify it in euphemistically sociolinguistic terms.

(1990, pp. 8–9)

The citation above represents the apex of Quirk's predicament. In only a few lines, it encapsulates all the major statements of the purist stance:

- outside the Inner Circle, English was used in an imperfect way;
- such imperfection was due to the interferences of local languages and cultures, which tainted the English language and made it deviate from the correct standard;
- it was therefore imperative that linguists and pedagogues alike abandon any propensity towards tolerance for such substandard forms of English in order to guarantee that learners were taught the best English possible.

It also epitomises a deep-seated attitude:

- variation in the English language resulting from non-Anglosaxon input was automatically seen as bearing the mark of deficit (as opposed to variation among Inner-Circle varieties);
- it was deemed sufficient to single out or even invent one sentence supposedly typical of a non-Anglosaxon English in order to support the notion that all non-Anglosaxon Englishes were always and incontestably deficient;
- there was profound antipathy towards sociolinguistics and, presumably, any branch of linguistics influenced by social sciences, and a predilection for building arguments and reaching conclusions on the basis of anecdotal evidence and personal impressions.

By this time, Quirk had fully embraced Prator's views and even adopted similarly colourful rhetoric: what the American linguist called a heresy, Quirk named a "half-baked quackery" (1990, p. 9). That was very unfortunate. By joining the "Pratorian guard" and assuming its intolerant attitude, picturesque style and disdain for empirical data, Quirk lost credibility. What was particularly regrettable was the fact that although he did raise some interesting issues, these were obscured by the overall tone and attitudinal orientation of his paper. I shall return to this point in more detail later.

Quirk's radicalised position was inevitably an invitation to criticism. Kachru did respond. In his usual lucid and incisive style, he pointed out the theoretical and attitudinal flaws in Quirk's paper and reiterated the importance of taking into account the "linguistic, sociolinguistic, educational and pragmatic realities" of multilingual societies when describing issues related to the spread of English worldwide (1991, pp. 6–7). He also underlined the urgency to dispel certain misconceptions in the field: that there is a causal link between learning English and wishing to interact with native speakers and to understand their culture, that non-native varieties of English are interlanguages and that native speakers play a primary role in the diffusion of the English language (1991, p. 10). This was part of a broader paradigm shift that Kachru had been advocating for years (Kachru, 1976, 1982, 1985, 1988a, 1988b). Fundamentally – and this was Kachru's main criticism of Quirk's paper – the view that non-native varieties of English were imperfect imitations of native varieties had to give way to a more realistic perspective, whereby language variation would be seen as part of ongoing processes of nativisation and acculturation of English worldwide.

I would contend that the *English Today* debate marked a very important point in the overall evolution of the field of EIW. This is for two reasons. First of all, in academic terms, the debate indicated quite clearly the defeat of the purist and vehemently conservative stance. Quirk's paper was, in this sense, more self-harming than persuasive. Indeed, he, like Prator 20 years earlier, was reacting, with some anxiety, to the pluralistic view of English that was conspicuously affirming itself in academia, developed and promoted not only by Braj Kachru but also, if with differences in emphasis, by an increasingly large number of applied linguists, such as, among others, Peter Strevens, Tom McArthur, Manfred Görlach and Jenny Cheshire. By the early 1990s, the contention was clearly an unequal one and the *English Today* debate sealed the academic victory of the many Englishes over one English.

The other reason why the Quirk–Kachru debate was important is that for the first time ideology was referred to explicitly as an important factor in the equation. Quirk criticised the tolerant attitude to language variation as an expression of a particular ideological stance which held that the notions of standard English and of (in)correct use were against personal liberty; he therefore branded this ethos "liberation linguistics". Quirk believed that tolerance towards varieties of English was a direct manifestation of such an ideological attitude and hence lacked appropriate theoretical underpinnings. Kachru did not entirely refute the accusation but remarked that Quirk himself could not be free of ideology, since "it is rare that there is a position without an ideological backdrop" (1991, p. 4).

If ideology was previously something that could be inferred implicitly (even if sometimes quite clearly), it was now indicated explicitly as one of the layers in the texture of the discourse about English in the world. The ideological layer, however, had in itself at least two finer substrata. On one level, it was conservatism versus liberalism, that is, the importance to retain a common standard versus the importance to guarantee that individuals had the freedom to use 'deviant' forms of English as long as intelligibility was intact and communication unimpeded. This was the main sense that Quirk had attributed to the term "liberation linguistics". On another level, the question had more profound implications, as it concerned not just language as such but views of the world. It was the First World versus the Third World or, to be more precise, the Third World's struggle to readjust the global equilibrium of power and reach effective independence after the long colonial period. Quirk himself had alluded to this: "English was indeed the language used by men like Gandhi and Nehru in the movement to liberate India from the British raj and it is not surprising that 'liberation linguistics' should have a very special place in relation to such countries" (1990, p. 8). In this sense, freedom to use different forms of English was not the expression of a linguistic caprice, nor was it based on the more serious notion that communication is not necessarily impeded by the use of non-standard forms. Instead, it was an integral part of the process for former British colonies to regain independent national identities. This was a cardinal point in Kachru's position:

> As an exponent of cultural and ideological contact and change, the English language has acquired two faces: One representing the 'Westerness', the Judeo-Christian tradition; the other [...] reflecting the non-Western identities. The second face of English – the more obscure face – reflects what for some is the elusive concept of Asian or African identities, or the Third World identities.
>
> (1988b, p. 4)

In his responses to Prator and to Quirk, and indeed in the entirety of his work, Kachru strived to make the "second face of English" less obscure and the concept of Third World identities less elusive. In this sense, Kachru aligned himself with the sociopolitical discourse of Edward Said (1978) and Homi Bhabha (1990, 1994) and it is without doubt that a decentralised, pluralistic and egalitarian view of English is now the dominant one within applied linguistics. This is, primarily, an anti-imperialistic ideological stance.

3.4   The anti-imperialism of world Englishes

As was discussed in the previous sections, the *leitmotif* in much WE literature has been the necessity to grant equal status to forms of English outside and beyond the confines of Britain and America. Referring to the newly rebranded journal *World Englishes* in 1985, Tom McArthur commented that *world Englishes* and its acronym *WE* highlighted the idea of "a club of equals" and of "the democratization of attitudes to English everywhere on the globe" (1987, p. 334). It was clear that the suffix *-es* attached to *English* was not a purely descriptive grammatical item, but was accompanied by the idea that these Englishes should be seen as equal to one another. In outlining the aims of their book, Platt et al. stressed that they hoped to show *"above all*, the legitimacy" of new Englishes (1984, p. vii, my emphasis). Such statements were indicative of a clear will to achieve an objective above and beyond mere language description. Indeed, the idea was that language description could be used as a vehicle to the demonstration of language equality. In part, that objective has been achieved, at least within academic circles, where the necessity to affirm the legitimacy and equality of non-British and non-American varieties of English stemmed from an antipathy towards dismissive attitudes that had been expressed towards such varieties in certain quarters of applied linguistics.

But language *per se* was not the real problem. Languages are not 'things' that can be objectified and assessed on the basis of non-existent intrinsic qualities; they cannot be the subject of value judgements. All languages are integral to the lives of those who use them. Therefore, anything said about the 'value' or the 'quality' of any language cannot escape being, really, about its *users*. Even a seemingly harmless or positive comment such as 'Italian is a musical language' implies the presumed existence of certain characteristics of Italian people (e.g. a special innate artistic disposition). So, as language is never divorced from the people who use it, the "club of equals" did not refer only to varieties of English as such but also, and primarily, to *users* of English. Again, this was in response to a general attitude according to which language varieties do differ in quality and value. Such an attitude was expressed through explicitly negative evaluative comments such as this:

I am firmly convinced that for the rest of the English-speaking world the most unintelligible educated variety is Indian English. The national group that profits least from [...] efforts to improve their intelligibility by classroom instruction also seems to be the Indians; they can almost never be brought to believe that there is any reason for trying to change their pronunciation.

(Prator, 1968, p. 473)

There is an unequivocal value judgement here, both about Indian English as a variety and about the *users* of Indian English. It would have been very difficult not to respond to such statements. And much of the academic endeavour in WE can be read precisely as a response to that kind of affirmations, which seemed to echo nineteenth-century imperialist discourse about the superiority of European culture over any other culture. For the sake of comparison, it is worth citing a section of Macaulay's notorious 'Minute on Education' (1835), about the differences in quality between European and Indian languages and cultures:

[…] the dialects commonly spoken among the natives of this part of India, contain neither literary nor scientific information, and are, moreover, so poor and rude that, until they are enriched from some other quarter, it will not be easy to translate any valuable work into them. It seems to be admitted on all sides, that the intellectual improvement of those classes of the people who have the means of pursuing higher studies can at present be effected only by means of some language not vernacular amongst them.

What then shall that language be? One-half of the Committee maintain that it should be the English. The other half strongly recommend the Arabic and Sanscrit. The whole question seems to me to be, which language is the best worth knowing?

I have no knowledge of either Sanscrit or Arabic. But I have done what I could to form a correct estimate of their value. I have read translations of the most celebrated Arabic and Sanscrit works. I have conversed both here and at home with men distinguished by their proficiency in the Eastern tongues. I am quite ready to take the Oriental learning at the valuation of the Orientalists themselves. I have never found one among them who could deny that a single shelf of a good European library was worth the whole native literature of India and Arabia. The intrinsic superiority of the Western literature is, indeed, fully admitted by those members of the Committee who support the Oriental plan of education.

> It will hardly be disputed, I suppose, that the department of lit-
> erature in which the Eastern writers stand highest is poetry. And
> I certainly never met with any Orientalist who ventured to main-
> tain that the Arabic and Sanscrit poetry could be compared to that of
> the great European nations. But when we pass from works of imagi-
> nation to works in which facts are recorded, and general principles
> investigated, the superiority of the Europeans becomes absolutely
> immeasurable. It is, I believe, no exaggeration to say, that all the
> historical information which has been collected from all the books
> written in the Sanscrit language is less valuable than what may be
> found in the most paltry abridgements used at preparatory schools
> in England. In every branch of physical or moral philosophy, the
> relative position of the two nations is nearly the same.

Language is used here as a metonymy for *culture* and, eventually, *people*.
Indeed, Macaulay's 'Minute' should be read as part of the more general
narrative aimed at providing a moral justification to colonialism by portraying the Empire as a provider of civilisation. For that reason it was
important to discredit the colonies' cultures, religions, literatures and
languages.

Even if they were made in different context and certainly did not
reach the level of Macaulay's openly racist remarks, Prator's assertions
seemed to exhibit a certain continuity of attitude, as if they had been
somehow inspired by the same imperialist ethos. Thus, the strong disapproval and rejection of the 'purist' stance that was eventually expressed
in applied linguistics was essentially based on anti-imperialist principles.
The egalitarian and democratic view of the English language that began
to be voiced in the 1960s was underpinned by, and part of, a more general decentralised view of the world, whereby wealth and power should
be equally distributed. Therefore, it can be said that the WE paradigm
was originally articulated on the basis of an ideological, anti-imperialist
position.

Within this general context, an important source of inspiration for the
WE school of thought that emerged in the 1970s was the debate that had
begun to unfold in postcolonial literature about the roles of the English
language. A brief review of that debate will be useful at this point.

3.5   The location and relocation of English in postcolonial literature

In the immediate wake of independence, the location of English in
the former colonies was an uncomfortable one. There was desire and

necessity to express Asian, African and Caribbean identities from Asian, African and Caribbean perspectives but there was controversy over which language, English or vernaculars, should be used for such expression. A central point of discussion was whether political independence corresponded to equivalent forms of linguistic independence. According to Burchfield,

> There are no constitutional processes leading to declarations of linguistic independence as there are in politics. No flags are run up as signs or symbols of linguistic sovereignty.
>
> (1985, p. 160)

So the English language became the subject of two opposite attitudes in the former colonies: abrogation and appropriation. These attitudes existed both at the political level and at the literary level. The roles of English in the postcolonial world and the postcolonial world's attitudes and responses to the linguistic legacy of the British Empire have been the subject of a large volume of academic work (see, among many others, Ashcroft et al., 1989; Walder, 1998; Talib, 2002; Boehmer, 2005; Innes, 2007). The use, or not, of the colonisers' language has been a bone of contention since even before political independence was attained. In this regard, the positions of Raja Rao, Gabriel Okara, Chinua Achebe, Ngũgĩ wa Thiong'o and Salman Rushdie are among the most frequently cited and most representative. Raja Rao was the first English-using Indian writer to acquire international fame. His comments on the adoption of English in the foreword to his novel *Kanthapura* have become a classic in postcolonial literary studies:

> The telling has not been easy. One has to convey in a language that is not one's own; the spirit that is one's own. One has to convey the various shades and omissions of a certain thought-movement that looks maltreated in an alien language. I use the word 'alien', yet English is not really an alien language to us. It is the language of our intellectual make-up, like Sanskrit or Persian was before, but not of our emotional make-up. We are all instinctively bilingual, many of us writing in our own language and in English. We cannot write like the English. We should not. We cannot write only as Indians. We have grown to look at the large world as part of us. Our method of expression therefore has to be a dialect which will some day prove to be as distinctive and colourful as the Irish or the American. Time alone will justify it.
>
> (Rao, 1938, p. vii)

Rao identified key issues: language ownership; the ambivalent nature of English in postcolonial settings, in search of a balance between the roles of imperialist language, national language and international language; and the necessity of forging a distinctive variety of English. This last aspect was discussed by Nigerian writer Gabriel Okara, who believed that the essence of African ideas, cultures and values could be expressed through English only if it were suitably reshaped for that purpose. According to Okara, the mere fact of being an African was not enough in order to express African-ness if one was to write in English. What African writers needed was "a conscious effort to make [their] writing African through the use of words or the construction of sentences" (1963, p. 15). So, in order to make one's writing truly African, Okara felt that it was necessary to translate words and phrases as faithfully as possible from African languages into English:

> As a writer who believes in the utilisation of African ideas, African philosophy and African folk-lore and imagery to the fullest extent possible, I am of the opinion that the only way to use them effectively is to translate them almost literally from the African language native to the writer into whatever European language he is using as his medium of expression.
>
> (1963, p. 15)

After providing a few examples of direct translation of salutations from the Ijaw and the Ibo languages into English, he argued that "a writer can use the idioms of his own language in a way that is understandable in English" and that "[i]f he uses their English equivalents, he would not be expressing African ideas and thoughts, but English ones" (1963, p. 15). Okara observed that although expressions such as "may we live to see ourselves tomorrow" and "may it dawn" – both the social equivalents of "goodnight" – may be regarded by some as "a desecration of the [English] language", they were in fact indicative of the dynamism and malleability of English and all languages:

> Living languages grow like living things, and English is far from a dead language. There are American, West Indian, Australian, Canadian, and New Zealand versions of English. All of them add life and vigour to the language while reflecting their own respective cultures. Why shouldn't there be a Nigerian or West African English which we

can use to express our own ideas, thinking and philosophy in our own way?

(1963, p. 16)

Even though it may sound like a mechanistic linguistic exercise, Okara's idea of faithful translation was underpinned by the fundamental and more general principle that English needed a certain amount of modification in order to express genuine African-ness. The same notion was expressed by fellow Nigerian Chinua Achebe, who framed his argument more firmly within issues of postcolonial identity and cultural independence:

> Those of us who have inherited the English language may not be in a position to appreciate the value of the inheritance [...]. Or we may go on resenting it because it came as part of a package deal which included many other items of doubtful value and the positive atrocity of racial arrogance and prejudice which may yet set the world on fire. But let us not in reflecting the evil throw out the good with it.
>
> (1965, p. 28)

Achebe was a strong believer in the pragmatic benefits of using a world language rather than a vernacular language. He did not criticise those who chose not to use English, nor did he feel that their work was in any way less valuable and worthy of admiration. However, he contended that the main disadvantage of local languages was that they were not used widely enough and literary works written in them would inevitably suffer from being inaccessible by those who were unable to read them. He therefore explained his linguistic choice very clearly:

> The real question is not whether Africans could write in English but whether they ought to. Is it right that a man should abandon his mother-tongue for someone else's? It looks like a dreadful betrayal and produces a guilty feeling. But for me there is no other choice. I have been given this language and I intend to use it.
>
> (1965, p. 30)

Like Okara, Achebe felt the need to forge an English that would be suitable in conveying the African writer's experience:

> [M]y answer to the question, Can an African ever learn English well enough to be able to use it effectively in creative writing? is certainly

yes. If on the other hand you ask: Can he ever learn to use it like a native speaker? I should say: I hope not. It is neither necessary nor desirable for him to be able to do so. The price a world language must be prepared to pay is submission to many different kinds of use. The African writer should aim to use English in a way that brings out his message best without altering the language to the extent that its value as a medium of international exchange will be lost. He should aim at fashioning out an English which is at once universal and able to carry his peculiar experience.

[...]

I feel that the English language will be able to carry the weight of my African experience. But it will have to be a new English, still in full communion with its ancestral home but altered to suit its new African surroundings.

(1965, pp. 29–30)

Achebe's words echo both Rao's and Okara's. His position epitomises what Ashcroft et al. (1989) called the "appropriation" of English, that is, the idea that the English language could be maintained and adopted by creative writers in former British colonies despite the fact that it arrived there together with imperialism, provided that it was some-how modified, localised and thus stripped of its colonial connotations. The opposite of appropriation was "abrogation", namely, the rejection of English on the grounds that its continued presence in postcolonial settings was incompatible with the attainment of a full political and cultural independence from the former colonisers. Kenyan writer Ngũgĩ wa Thiong'o expressed this sentiment very clearly when he explained the reasons why he decided to stop writing in English and to use a local Kenyan language in his literary work:

I started writing in Gĩkũyũ language in 1977 after seventeen years of involvement in Afro-European literature, in my case Afro-English literature.

[...]

I believe that my writing in Gĩkũyũ language, a Kenyan language, an African language, is part and parcel of the anti-imperialist struggles of Kenyan and African peoples.

(1986, pp. 27–28)

For Ngũgĩ, English was as a foreign language, and not just any foreign language, but one which had been imposed upon the Kenyan education system during colonial times at the expense of local languages. He therefore felt that its adoption for literary purposes would represent a perpetuation of the imperialistic language policies that had previously devalued African languages such as Gĩkũyũ:

> The question is this: we as African writers have always complained about the neo-colonial economic and political relationship to Euro-America. Right. But by our continuing to write in foreign languages, paying homage to them, are we not on the cultural level continuing the neo-colonial slavish and cringing spirit? What is the difference between a politician who says Africa cannot do without imperialism and the writer who says Africa cannot do without European languages?
>
> (1986, p. 26)

It was necessary, therefore, to ensure that African writers would finally enrich African languages to the same degree in which European writers had enriched their own languages for centuries:

> We African writers are bound by our calling to do for our languages what Spencer, Milton and Shakespeare did for English; what Pushkin and Tolstoy did for Russian; indeed what writers in the world history have done for their languages [...].
>
> (1986, p. 29)

Since he emphasised so strongly the need to revalue and return dignity to African languages, Ngũgĩ categorically refuted Okara's and Achebe's idea of forging a new English that would be able to express African-ness. English, for Ngũgĩ, was an alien language in Africa.

Salman Rushdie addressed exactly the same issues as those raised by Ngũgĩ, but from a diametrically opposite perspective. He defended the legitimacy of using English in literature produced by writers from post-colonial countries, arguing that considering English-language Indian writing a mere "post-colonial anomaly, the bastard child of Empire, sired on India by the departing British" was based on "the false premise that English, having arrived from outside India, is and must necessarily remain an alien there" (1997, p. xii). For Rushdie, English is an Indian language, and its local naturalisation can be compared to that of Urdu:

> Urdu, the camp-argot of the country's earlier Muslim conquerors, became a naturalised sub-continental language long ago; and by now that has happened to English, too. English has become an Indian

language. Its colonial origins mean that, like Urdu and unlike all other Indian languages, it has no regional base; but in all other ways, it has emphatically come to stay.

(1997, pp. xii–xiii)

He shares Achebe's view that local varieties of English need not be identical to British English: "Indian English, sometimes unattractively called 'Hinglish', is not 'English' English, to be sure, any more than Irish or American or Caribbean English is" so that writers can find their own "literary voices as distinctively Indian, and also as suitable for any and all of the purposes of art, as those other Englishes forged in Ireland, Africa, the West Indies and the United States" (1997, p. xiii). He takes issue with the critics who accuse the choice of using English as a form of neo-imperialism:

> [T]hese criticisms [...] are about class, power and belief. There is a whiff of political correctness about them: the ironical proposition that India's best writing since Independence may have been done in the language of the departed imperialists is simply too much for some folks to bear. It ought not to be true, and so must not be permitted to be true. (That many of the attacks on English-language Indian writing are made in English by writers who are themselves members of the college-educated, English-speaking elite is a further irony.)
>
> (1997, p. xiv)

Rushdie observes that through the use of English, Indian writers have been able to attain international reputation and this seems to have contributed significantly to turning the power balance between the West and the East: "[W]hat seems to be the case is that Western publishers and critics have been growing gradually more and more excited by the voices emerging from India [...]. It feels as if the East is imposing itself on the West, rather than the other way around" (1997, p. xiv).

The ideas and attitudes towards the English language expressed by Rao, Okara, Achebe, Rushdie and many more represent the essence of the concept of "writing back", which has focussed on the repossession of one's own identity also through the use of a reforged English:

> The language I speak
> Becomes mine, its distortions, its queernesses,
> All mine, mine alone.
>
> (from 'An Introduction', by Kamala Das)

The "distortions" of English were instrumental in what was effectively equivalent to a declaration of linguistic independence and linguistic sovereignty. The main idea was that the cultural appropriation of English could be attained primarily through the deliberate alteration of its code. It was one way to ensure that the imperial legacy of English would be removed or at least diminished: if writers made their language sufficiently and visibly different from that of their former colonisers, they would no longer be using a British language but a language that would be rid of the imperialistic negative connotations while, at the same time, retaining the intelligibility that is necessary and desirable in a language of international currency. Literary writers took upon themselves the task of resolving an ideological impasse by attempting to relocate the former colonisers' language through modifications of its shape.

Linguistic independence was a necessary component of political independence and, more in general, of a process of readjustment, if only very partial, of the power equilibrium of the world. It was important that the newly established self-governing countries be granted status and dignity equal to those of their former colonisers. Interestingly, British colonies regained their independence at a time when, or shortly after, human rights had been declared to be of universal validity: the first article of the United Nations' *Universal Declaration of Human Rights* (1948) stated that "All human beings are born free and equal in dignity and rights." The freedom of countries and of people was sought during centuries of struggle and when it was achieved, it needed to be declared officially. Recognition was fundamental. This was the historical and political background that a few decades later came to be a primary frame of reference for the philosophy and the discourse of the WE school of thought.

3.6   The ideological locus of world Englishes

To summarise: WE discourse developed as a response to purist stances about varieties of English and, at the same time, drew part of its ideological position from postcolonial literary discourse. In turn, purist positions were expressed in a rhetoric which contained echoes of the imperialist narrative on language and culture, while the postcolonial language debate was centred upon clear anti-imperialist concerns in the uneasy decision to adopt and alter the English language and echoed the nationalist language ideology discussed in Chapter 2. The place of the academic field of WE within this discoursal matrix can be represented diagrammatically as shown in Figure 3.1.

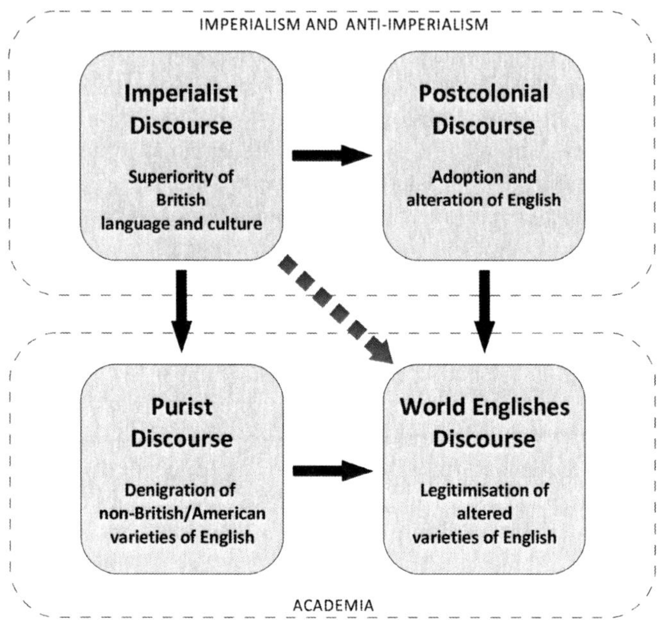

Figure 3.1   The ideological locus of world Englishes

The diagram establishes the ideological locus of WE, its opposition to the purist stance and ideological contiguity with the appropriation of English in postcolonial literary discourse. Mesthrie and Bhatt state that "The idea that the grammar of English emanates from the royal court of London has long been questioned in Linguistics and is being pushed to its limits in World Englishes studies" (2008, p. 26). This citation is one of the most efficiently concise and accurate descriptions of the WE rubric. First of all, the spatial reference to the royal court of London is highly significant: it represents the innermost point of the Inner Circle, the centre of Teaching English to Speakers of Other Languages (TESOL) and also the centre of power of the former empire. By challenging the authority of 'London', WE studies attempt to weaken the link between the English language and its historical capital. Secondly, the authority being challenged is that of the norm provider for the grammar of English. Grammar thus acquires a larger symbolic value, that of a metaphorical weapon, as has been eloquently expressed by John Agard in a poem voicing the social struggle of a Caribbean immigrant in London:

> I ent have no gun
> I ent have no knife

but mugging de Queen's English
is the story of my life
I dont need no axe
to split / up yu syntax
I dont need no hammer
to mash up yu grammar.

(from 'Listen Mr Oxford
don', by John Agard)

However, the collocation of the WE paradigm with postcolonial literary discourse presents a conceptual conundrum. Namely, the anti-imperialist drive founded on the idea of a plurality of Englishes is inherently contradictory as it is based on a fundamentally Eurocentric view of the world. This point will be illustrated and discussed in Chapter 4.

4
The Contradiction of Plurality

> …each nation believes in the superiority of its own idiom and is quick to regard the man who uses a different language as incapable of speaking.
>
> —Ferdinand de Saussure

4.1 Introduction

In the speech he delivered on the day India gained its independence from Britain, 15 August 1947, the first Indian Prime Minister Jawaharlal Nehru said the following:

> A moment comes, but rarely in history, when we step out from the old to the new, when an age ends, and when the soul of a nation, long suppressed, finds utterance.

The passage may be seen to encapsulate a condemnation of imperialism, the momentousness of the transition from colony to independent country and the importance for a nation to find its own utterance, its own mode of expression. By extension, it also condenses the essence of the WE ethos, according to which each variety of English represents a way for each former colony of the British Empire to find its own individual way of expressing itself in the language that was left by the colonisers. As Hickey remarks,

> There is no doubt […] that the 'World Englishes' enterprise […] is often about a perceived aim of decolonising English or deculturising English outside the 'Western World' in a vein similar to that in which postcolonial studies in literature and anthropology operates.
>
> (2004, p. 504)

As was seen in Chapter 3, scholars in the sociolinguistic field of 'World Englishes' highlight distinctive linguistic features characterising Outer-Circle varieties of English in an effort to demonstrate the acculturation of the language and the normative independence of such varieties from British and American English. Such distinctiveness is seen as the result of the re-rooting of English in different sociolinguistic realities, rather than an indication of imperfect command of the language. For this reason, Outer-Circle varieties of English should be considered on a par with any other variety in terms of quality and dignity. The outcome is a catalogue of Englishes named after the countries in which they are located. Such a classification is meant to represent a 'club of equals'.

This chapter argues that despite having had the great merit of bringing to the fore important sociolinguistic issues relating to the worldwide spread of English, the WE paradigm is caught in an ideological conundrum in which while it pursues its anti-imperialistic and egalitarian objectives, it actually replicates, and contributes to reinforcing, a view of the English language which stems directly from those very Eurocentric and imperialistic roots that it wishes to oppose. Thus, the WE paradigm is not only unable to achieve its purported aim, but the conceptualisation of English that it articulates actually leads to conclusions that turn that objective on its head.

This happens primarily for three interrelated reasons:

- the terminology and, more in general, the semiotics of WE are excessively simple and therefore incapable to capture and convey the complex meanings in the WE discourse;
- the identification and categorisation of varieties of English along national borders and the use of the three-circle (Inner, Outer and Expanding Circles) model have oversimplified the sociolinguistic realities of many areas of the world on the basis of the European modernist concept of nation-state;
- emphasis on linguistic difference among varieties of English has made it easier to posit ranking orders of 'quality' and to stigmatise varieties of English tagged with such modifiers as 'Third World', 'non-native', 'periphery', 'new' and so on.

4.2   The semiotics of world Englishes

Bolton (2006a, p. 240) notes that "The expression 'world Englishes' is capable of a range of meanings and interpretations" and illustrates this point by reviewing the major academic approaches in the field. The choice of the adjective "capable" is crucial here, as it implies that the term possesses an intrinsic semantic value, an in-built semiosis. My argument in this section is that the term *world Englishes* as well as the related verbal and visual signs normally used in the relevant literature to describe those meanings and interpretations are too simple and do not, in fact, possess the necessary semantic capability.

The semiotics of the WE paradigm is based on a fairly small set of primary signs:

World Englishes

Verbal signs
- world Englishes (or new Englishes)
- varieties of English
- the actual nomenclature of varieties of English (e.g. Nigerian English, Indian English, etc.)

Verbo-visual signs
- graphical representations of the spread of English, such as Kachru's three-circle model.

4.2.1   The verbal signs

Plurality is a central concept in WE. Its primal importance is signalled by the grammatically deviant form *Englishes* of the otherwise uncountable noun *English*. In academia, the word *Englishes* gained wider currency in the mid-1980s. In the seminal *The New Englishes*, Platt et al. provided the first account of the "diversity, the systematicity [and] the legitimacy of some of the New Englishes" (1984, p. vii). In his account of the English language, Burchfield (1985) dedicated a chapter to "dispersed forms of English", in which he provided an overview of different varieties based on distinctive linguistic features in them. Such varieties of English were primarily identified according to geographical location, and adjectives derived from country names were used as premodifiers to identify the different Englishes. As McArthur has observed, it was "[t]he regular and increasing uses of expressions like 'American English', 'Indian English', 'Scottish English', 'British English'" (1987, p. 33) that lead to the grammatical pluralisation of the word *English*.

These models imply that (a) there are as many different Englishes as there are countries in which English is used and (b) in each one of these countries, English displays certain distinctive features of phonology, lexis, grammar and so on so that British English is used in Britain, American English in America, Indian English in India and so on. In this sense, they are perfectly in line with the definition of *Englishes* in the Oxford English Dictionary: "regional varieties of English considered together, often in contradistinction to the concept of English as a language with a single standard or correct form." Correspondingly, when used within the phrase *world Englishes* the most obvious and common interpretation of the foregrounded plural is the idea that "English is not monolithic. Rather, there is a family of many different Englishes" (Hitchings, 2008, p. 339) in different parts of the world. One of the main tenets in WE literature is that the English language has diversified into a number of varieties as a result of its spread and its acculturation in different settings:

> The spread of a natural human language across the countries and regions of the planet has resulted in variation as a consequence of nativization and acculturation of the language in various communities [...]. These processes have affected the grammatical structure and the use of language according to the local needs and conventions.
>
> (Y. Kachru and Smith, 2008, p. 177)

Such variation concerns aspects of the language such as its "sounds, rhythm, words, processes of word formation, phrases, sentence patterns, idioms and metaphors, and discourse structures and strategies", as well as its "varied genres, conventions of politeness, code-mixing and switching, and new canons of literary creativity" (p. 177). As Kumaravadivelu explains, it is a process of reconstruction of a foreign language into a local one:

> Varieties such as Indian English, Nigerian English and Singaporean English represent the extent to which a foreign language can be profitably reconstructed into a vehicle for expressing sociocultural norms and networks that are typically local.
>
> (Kumaravadivelu, 2003, p. 539)

However, this fairly straightforward concept represents only a subsection of the full semantics of 'world Englishes'. As Benson points out, the term 'world Englishes' refers to "a complex multidimensional construct involving pragmatic, sociolinguistic, and literary dimensions" as opposed to "the simplistic view that each English-using region has its own distinctive 'English' belonging to its inhabitants and describable in terms of formal linguistic variation" (2005, p. 378). From this perspective, formal linguistic variation constitutes only one of what Bolton has called "interlocking models of World Englishes" (2003, p. 37). Thus, this means that if the idea of plural Englishes has to do with more than just linguistic features, the notion 'English' necessarily extends beyond language. This creates "a tension between what are seen as the organic qualities of dialects and varieties as the 'natural' expression of vital linguistic systems, and the view of languages and language varieties as social and political constructs" (Bolton, 2006b, p. 308). It seems to me that the difference between these two interpretations is of fundamental importance.

In the editorial of the first issue of the journal *World Englishes*, Kachru and Smith explained that " 'Englishes' symbolizes the *functional* and formal variation in the language" (1985, p. 210, my emphasis). The functional type of variation adds a very important element to the equation and raises its degree of complexity quite significantly. It applies on an international scale as well as on a national scale. Internationally, the notion of functional variation refers to the fact that English is used

- as a national language in countries where it is the first (and, often, only) language for the majority of the population;
- as a national language in countries where it is an additional language alongside other local languages;
- as a lingua franca for international communication.

Moving down from the level of international functional variation to the level of intranational functional variation (particularly in Outer-Circle settings), Kachru has made more delicate distinctions according to the roles that English plays in education, in administration, as a *super partes* national lingua franca, as a literary language and so on. The use of English in various domains is what Kachru has termed the *range* of a particular variety of English. In addition, the extent to which the use of English penetrates levels of society constitutes the *depth* dimension of functional variation (1986, pp. 91–96). These two dimensions could be plotted respectively on the vertical and the horizontal axes of a bi-dimensional graph. If, for instance, *depth* is based on levels of education, the resulting graph could look like the one in Figure 4.1.

Clearly, the one in Figure 4.1 is a very simplified diagram. The range of uses is far from complete, as more domains can be added, such as those of literature, media communication, commerce and so on. Additionally, the level of education is only one possible parameter of depth, social class being another obvious one. The additional diagram that would result if social class were to be considered would have to be stacked onto the first one in order to generate a more comprehensive picture, and the bi-dimensional graph would then become a tri-dimensional one. It

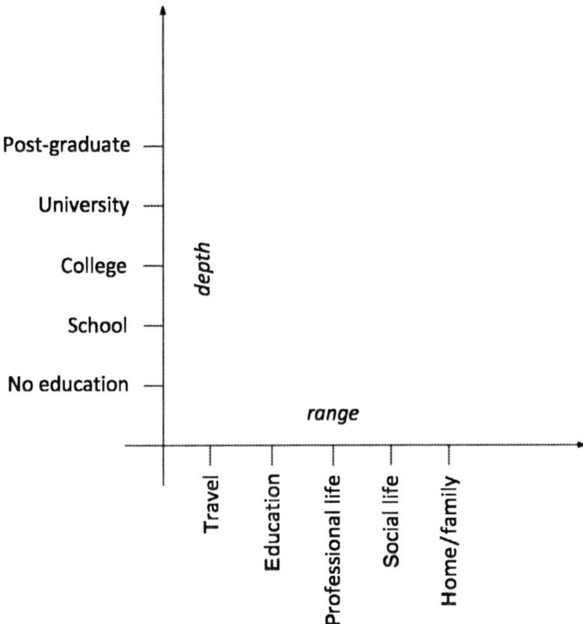

Figure 4.1   Axes of functional variation: Depth and range

is thus evident that functional variation is composed of an intricate set of variables and that a comprehensive analysis would have to take into account such complexity.

Figure 4.2 below shows a graphical representation that seeks to capture the main threads in the Kachruvian model of world Englishes. As the diagram shows, formal language variation is only a relatively small aspect in the Kachruvian model of world Englishes, which goes much further than locating varieties of English on the world map.

Indeed, the very concept of 'language variety' is intended in a multidimensional way. The typical sense that the word has in sociolinguistics is that of an umbrella term referring to forms of language variation typically called dialect, accent, style and register (see, among others, Trudgill, 2003) and generally conceived as being describable on the basis of the distribution of certain linguistic features, determined by regional, social or contextual variables. In the WE paradigm this linguistic sense of 'variety' is maintained, but it is also used in conjunction with other aspects of variation. For example, with reference to American English, but exemplifying all Englishes, Kachru has argued that "the distinctive uses of English in [...] America and resultant

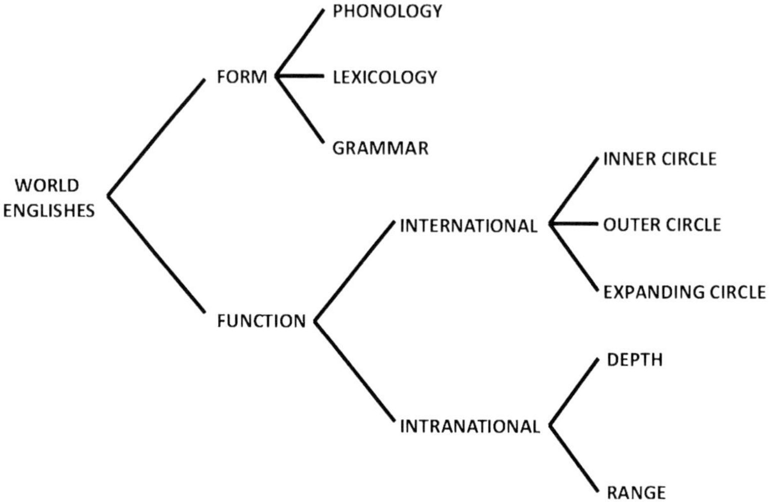

Figure 4.2   The interwoven threads of world Englishes

nativisation in American sociocultural (and linguistic) contexts contributed to its Americanness and make [*sic*] it in some respect separate from British English" (1981, p. 23). Similarly, a number of years later, and with reference to the South Asian context, he contended that "the South Asianness of English [...] has to be characterized both in terms of its linguistic characteristics and in terms of its contextual and pragmatic functions" (2005, p. 43). From this perspective, therefore, "variety of English" comes to acquire a significantly different meaning from the one normally attributed to the term elsewhere. That is, it is no longer, or not only, a form of English identifiable through a set of linguistic features but refers instead to the *incarnation* of English within a given society. Terms such as *Indian English, Singaporean English, Nigerian English* and so on do not merely designate particular linguistic codes as dialects of English, but are to be intended more holistically as the ways in which the English language is part of, and operates in, the sociocultural and linguistic realities of India, Singapore, Nigeria and so on. The central idea is that local identities

> have contributed to the English language a number of fascinating strands of multiculturalism, for example: (a) *Distinct cultural identity as a variety,* for example, Nigerian English, Singaporean English, and Indian English; (b) *Appropriate acculturation of the variety* in terms of sociocultural, religious, and interactional contexts;

(c) *Organization of discourse strategies and speech acts* which are distinct from the ones considered appropriate in the Inner Circle; and (d) *Alteration of linguistic codes* due to the multilingual contexts of the use of English. [...] It is through these underlying cultural, linguistic, and ideological contexts that English has gradually turned into Englishes thus acquiring a unique multiculturism, multicanons, and internationalism.

(Kachru, 1996)

There are clearly a multiplicity of layers here acting upon the concept of 'variety'. In highlighting the primary role of the sociocultural context in the production and analysis of language, Kachru follows the anthropological and linguistic tradition of Malinowski, Firth and Halliday. However, even within a theory of language as social semiotic, the very principle asserting that formal variation of the linguistic code results from variation in the sociocultural and linguistic context entails that the two types of variation are distinct phenomena. If contextual functional variation and linguistic variation are linked by a cause-and-effect relationship, the attribution of both to the single term *varieties of English* or *world Englishes* is semantically problematic. The resulting polysemy may well be indicative of the complexity of the phenomenon that the term seeks to encapsulate, but the excessive semantic stretch makes the intended meaning of *world Englishes* cognitively unmanageable and, therefore, rather opaque. The expanded conceptualisation of *world Englishes* cannot be adequately expressed by the term itself and the only interpretation that it is capable of is the simplistic, language-based interpretation that Benson alludes to.

4.2.2   The visual signs

The notion of linguistic variation encoded in the term *world Englishes* is one based on geography, and the geopolitical map of the world constitutes a convenient and ready-made graphical representation upon which varieties of English are categorised. In the 1980s, it was precisely the world map that formed the basis of influential models of English in the world (Figure 4.3).

Kachru himself has explained that apart from the historical context of the types of spread of English, the three circles also represent "the patterns of acquisition, the functional allocations and the ideational constructs of the language" (2005, p. 214). However, a relatively simple set of signs, three circles and three lists of countries with their respective populations (Figure 4.4), has been loaded with more meaning than they can reasonably be expected to express.

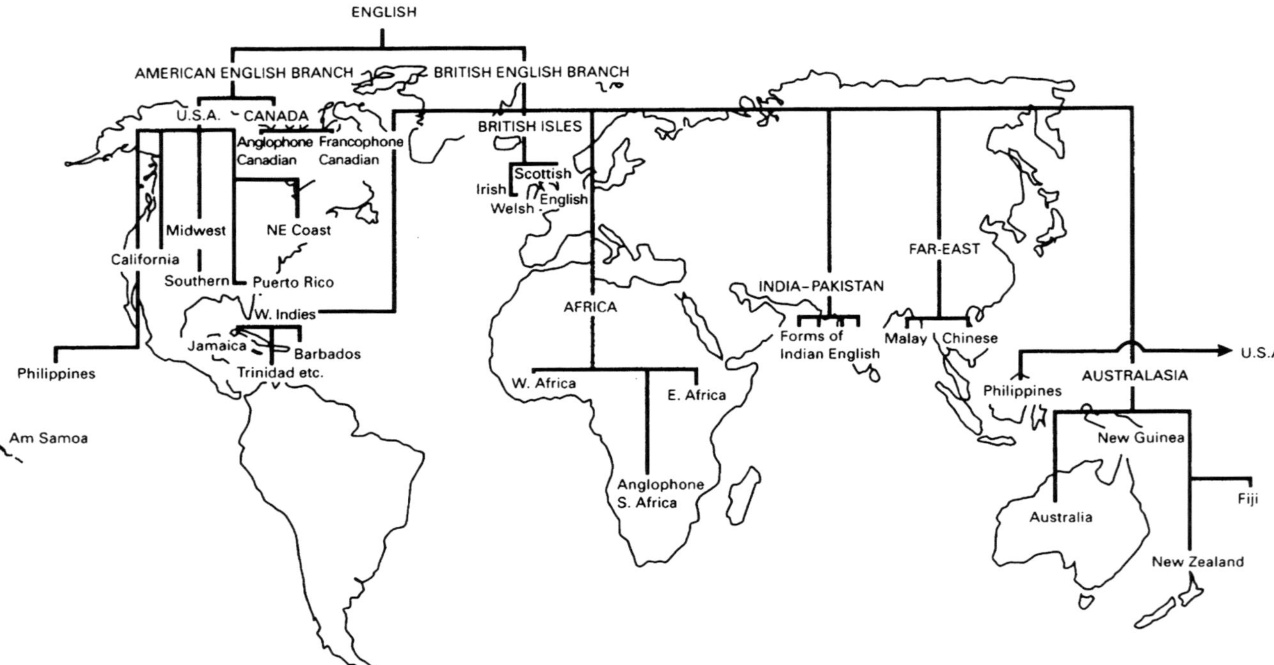

Figure 4.3 Models of English in the world: Strevens, Görlach and McArthur

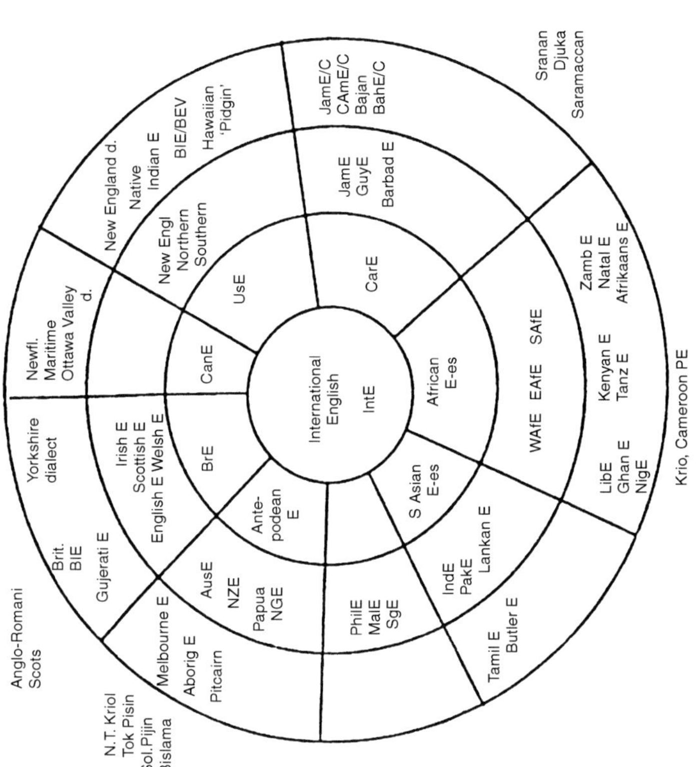

Figure 4.3 (Continued)

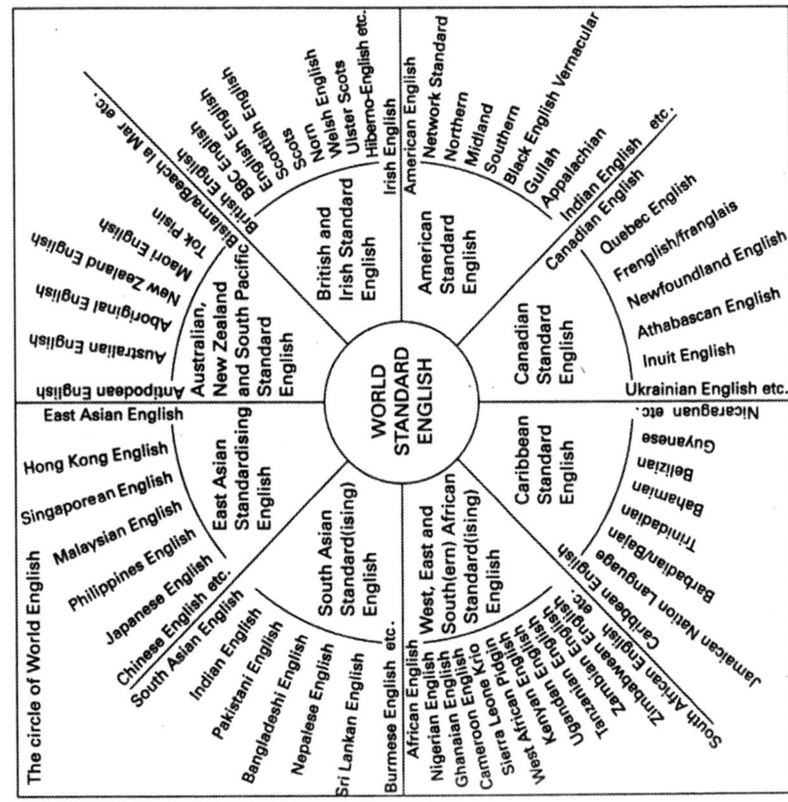

Figure 4.3 (Continued)

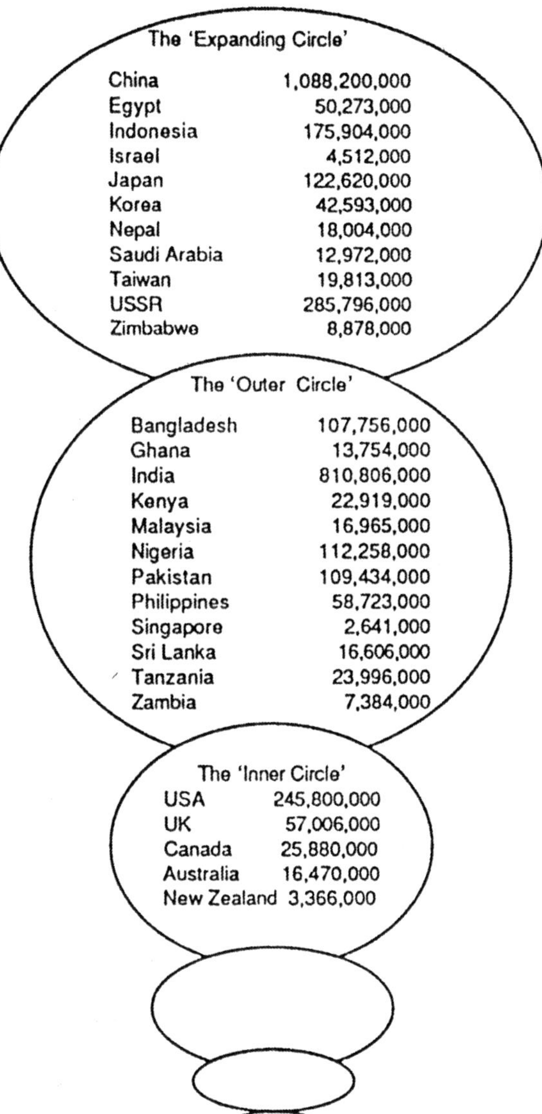

Figure 4.4   Kachru's three circles of English

Inevitably, the model has received criticism by a number of schol-ars, most prominently, Jenkins (2003), Bruthiaux (2003), Pennycook (2003, 2006, 2009) and Yano (2001, 2009), who have identified some shortcomings in its conceptualisation. Criticism has mostly focussed on the inability of the model to adequately represent change in the roles of English with respect to geographical location. Observ-ing, among other facts, that English is used as a first language by a growing number of people in the Outer Circle and that flows of immigration have significantly altered the linguistic repertoire in Inner-Circle countries, Yano contends that it is necessary to move "from the geography-based model to the person-based model of English speakers" (2009, p. 212).

It is clear that the rigidity of the model and the uniformities that it assumes cannot offer an accurate depiction of the use or the users of English in the world. Again, as is the case with the verbal signs *world Englishes* and *varieties of English,* the visual signs utilised in the WE discourse are excessively simple. For this reason, both Yano (2009) and Pennycook (2009) have proposed alternative, 'three-dimensional' models, trying to capture a fuller and more faithful representation of English use. For my part, one point that I wish to focus my attention on is related to the centrality of the Inner Circle, which is particularly apparent in the version of the diagram popularised by David Crystal (1997) (Figure 4.5). The issue has been raised by Jenkins:

> The term 'Inner Circle' implies that speakers from the ENL countries are central to the effort, whereas their world-wide influence is in fact in decline. (Note, though, that Kachru did not intend the term 'Inner' to be taken to imply any sense of superiority.)
>
> (2003, p. 18)

To this observation, Kachru has responded thus:

> The term 'inner' [...] does not indicate any 'superiority' but is intended to capture the historical source of the English language. The concept 'Concentric Circles' is, therefore, used to suggest the starting point in Britain for the stages of the diffusion of the language. In the spread of English, Britain [...] carried the banner of the English lan-guage to what is now Anglophone Asia and Africa, and the rest is a long history.
>
> (2005, p. 219)

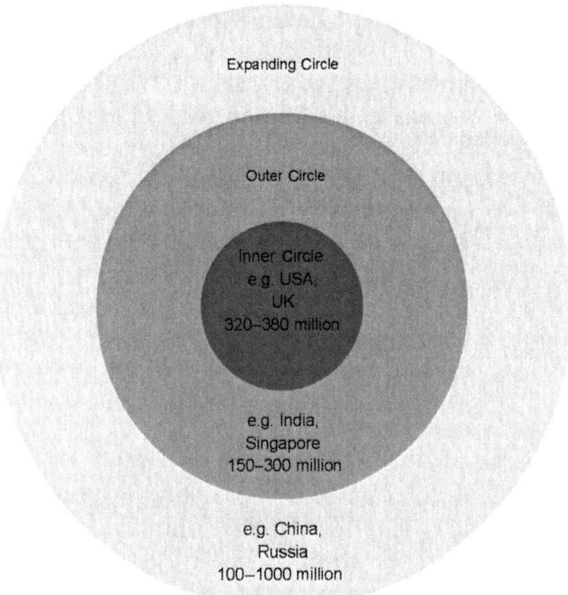

Figure 4.5   The concentric-circle model

It seems to me that the question is still unresolved. It is not so much because the worldwide influence of English as a Native Language (ENL) speakers may be in decline, but because of the highly symbolic meaning of the Inner Circle as a verbo-visual semiotic sign. The point that I wish to make is that even if 'Inner Circle' is not meant to indicate superiority, the fact remains that an author's intentions have limited power in shaping readers' interpretations. That is, it is difficult to disregard that both its physical position in the diagram and its name suggest that the Inner Circle designates a sort of elite group of Englishes and their users, clearly distinguished from the rest. Both the modifier *Inner* and the noun *Circle* connote the idea of an exclusive club to which entry is dreamed of but rarely granted. In addition, that the Inner Circle may capture the 'source' of the language is questionable not only from a historical point of view (New Zealand, for example, was colonised later than India was) but also from a linguistic one. The notion that a language may have an original source sees languages as objects that originate at a particular time and in a particular place, then grow, develop, perhaps are spread around by their speakers and perhaps eventually die. This conception of language as object will be discussed more in detail in Chapter 7, but it is worth pointing out here that the concept of a 'historical source' of English contributes to reinforcing the idea that Britain is indeed the location of the 'original' and, therefore, arguably the most authentic and purest form of English. Moreover, by grouping Australia, Canada, Ireland, New Zealand and the United States together with Britain, the Inner Circle becomes the location where people and places are culturally drawn together by a common Anglosaxon ancestry, the ancestral roots of English.

Wierzbicka (2006), for example, finds the three-circle model "pertinent and helpful" (p. 6) for her purpose of showing that there is a significant distinction between what she calls 'Anglo English', used by " 'Anglo Celtic' speakers of English – in Britain, the United States, and elsewhere" (p. 4), and other forms of English:

> In accordance with this distinction, we can say that, for example, Australian English – different as it is in many ways from both British and American English – belongs nonetheless to the inner circle, whereas, for example, Singapore English belongs to the outer one.
>
> (2006, p. 6)

And, as a natural consequence, Singaporean English is "more different from British English and American English than these two are from one another" (p. 6). Consequently, all descriptions of English and of its users outside the Inner Circle inevitably take this Anglosaxon exclusive club as the ultimate point of reference, since "to adequately characterize Englishes of the outer circle such as Singapore English and to fully understand them as expressions of local cultures, it is eminently useful to be able to compare and contrast them with Anglo English" (p. 6).

As Wierzbicka's statements show, the concentric-circle model also embodies another factor in the WE paradigm that has significantly contributed to preventing its own aims from being reached, namely, the identification of varieties of English within the political borders of different countries. As Alastair Pennycook has cogently observed,

> [the model] constructs speaker identity along national lines within these circles. [...] [T]his suggests that speakers within a country belong in a particular circle and speak a particular national variety (or don't, if their country happens to be in the rather large expanding circle) [...]. Thus language users are assigned to a particular variety of English according, on the one hand, to their nationality and, on

the other, to the location of that nation within a particular circle. Australians speak English as a native language, Malaysians speak it as a second language, and Japanese use it as a foreign language. The problem is that it depends very much who you are: a well-educated Chinese Malaysian in Kuala Lumpur may speak English as a 'second' or 'first' language, while a rural Malay may know English only as a distant foreign language. Parallel relations can be found in Australia and Japan, and indeed wherever we care to look around the world.

(2003, p. 519)

The examples cited by Pennycook of "a well-educated Chinese Malaysian in Kuala Lumpur" and "a rural Malay" are not to be taken as exceptions to the rule or, on the other extreme, as ethnic generalisations: they exemplify a sociolinguistic reality which is indeed observable "wherever we care to look around the world".

4.3   The nomenclature of world Englishes

Medgyes' statement that "there are as many equal varieties of English as there are countries where English is spoken as first or second language" (1992, p. 340) epitomises well one of the tenets in the WE literature, in which varieties of English are typically named after the countries with which they are associated. However, the idea that national borders coincide with linguistic borders presents fundamental difficulties:

In the first place the linguist may try to narrow down the scope of linguistic description geographically. Thus, if informants are chosen from particular regions, 'English' may be subdivided into American English, Australian English, Welsh English, Scottish English, etc., each being treated as a separate variety [...]. But this strategy brings problems in its turn. Within such broad groupings there are still geographically distinct variations (e.g. between New York and New Orleans, or between Bristol and Liverpool). [...]

A further weakness in attempts to pin down linguistic variation geographically arises from the fact that even when a very precise location is pinpointed for investigation it is commonly found that speech in the local community is far from uniform, varying according to such factors as age, sex and social strata of the speakers.

(Harris, 2001, p. 125)

The labelling of world Englishes on the basis of country names points towards the opposite direction. Namely, it suggests that the identification of varieties of English is not only possible but also a fairly straightforward process, as each one of them is located within the borders of the country that lends it its name. It also suggests that the "sociocultural norms and networks" (see Kumaravadivelu's citation above) that each English is associated with are demarcated by the borders of the country in which that English is said to be spoken (India, Singapore, Nigeria, etc.).

One problem with this form of identification of varieties of English is that it assumes sociocultural homogeneity in localities where different ethnic groups, religions, cultures and languages co-exist within the same national borders. Even a small country like Singapore has an extremely variegated demography, composed not only of its historical Chinese, Malay and South Indian base, but also of large numbers of migrant workers from nearby South and Southeast Asian countries, who contribute to the complex sociolinguistic reality of the country. Thus, sociocultural norms may indeed be local but the geographical spaces of their localities rarely correspond to the spaces delimited by national borders. Sociolinguistic realities are far more complex than what the neat country-based premodifiers used in the catalogue of Englishes suggest. The one-language–one-nation–one-country construct is inapplicable in most parts of the world, where multilingualism and multiculturalism are the norm.

Besides, the ways in which people use languages escape this type of compartmentalisations, and so do speech communities, which "may or may not be national" (Brutt-Griffler, 2002, p. 175). Indeed,

> [i]ndividuals may belong to several speech communities (which may be discrete or overlapping), just as they may participate in a variety of social settings. Which ones or one individuals orient themselves to at any given moment – which set of social and communicative rules they use – is part of the strategy of communication. To understand this phenomenon, one must recognize that each member of a community has a repertoire of social identities and that each identity in a given context is associated with a number of appropriate verbal and nonverbal forms of expression.
>
> (Saville-Troike, 1996, p. 357)

Groups and identities intersect, and the notion of "nested identities" (Herb and Kaplan, 1999) seems to be a more accurate representation. In addition, people's identities are not fixed:

[e]thnic identities [...] are not cast in stone. Who belongs to an ethnic group can change, as can how the ethnic group is known. People speaking the same language may not really identify with each other at one time but do so at another.

(Honey, 1999, p. 176)

Where it is used in these situations, English does often represent an intranational lingua franca, but this is the case only because it happens to be the only neutral, a-regional language available not associated with any particular cultural group. Also, the availability of English may be interregional and intercultural but rarely cuts across social classes, as it tends instead to remain the prerogative of a wealthy and well-educated elite. To what extent, therefore, English can be a truly national language is extremely difficult to say. That is why, with reference to the Ghanaian context, Anyidoho and Dakubu have commented that

Boadi's (1994: 56) statement that 'One hopes that...a standard Ghanaian English will emerge' is coherent only if a characteristically Ghanaian English is to be an index of Ghanaian national identity.

(2008, p. 144, n. 1)

The expression "one hopes" is interesting. Who exactly is *one*? And why do they *hope* that a standard Ghanaian (or any other) English will emerge, especially if the issue of Ghanaian national identity is not seriously considered? The impression is that through the classification of varieties of English, WE academics take upon themselves the task of creating connections of identity between suitably named Englishes and the nations that are presupposed to speak them. So the validity of the nomenclature of varieties of English is presented as a given, and the hope for a full recognition of national Englishes is a necessary consequence. With reference to Nigeria, Bamgboṣe has observed that

The English language has undergone modifications in the Nigerian environment. It has been pidginized, nativized, acculturated and twisted to express unaccustomed concepts and modes of interaction. As a result, it is now a Nigerian English at par with other World Englishes. [...] The challenge we face now is to intensify research on this English and codify it appropriately.

(1995, p. 26)

The logic flow is classic: the 'thing' Nigerian English has undergone the same process of acculturation as other Englishes have and it is the linguist's task to describe it rigorously and give it dignity by codification. This is presented as an unquestionably positive thing to do. Not everyone, however, shares the same conviction. A drastically more distrustful perception has been expressed by Krishnaswamy and Burde, who see the WE paradigm as a form of linguistic colonialism:

> Indian English, Pakistani English, Bangladeshi English, Sri Lankan English, Nepali English, Malaysian English. Singaporean English, Nigerian English, Ghanaian English, Filipino English, Fiji English, etc. Don't these look like the airlines of various countries – Air India. Pakistan International, Singapore Airlines etc. with the planes that are manufactured by one or two companies in the First World [...] and bought by these developing countries after getting the interior decoration done to reflect the local 'culture'? There are middlemen to do the lobbying and promote the sales and, more often than not, the agents are the non-resident natives of the countries that buy these products. These non-native lobbyists are encouraged and exhibited as show-pieces and 'tokens' of the native tolerance but every time a 'new brand' is floated there are more benefits and advantages to the country that exports the product. Some sort of nationalistic sentiment makes these consumer-countries use their own labels, and the business interests of the manufacturing companies and First World countries encourage the use of different brand-names for the same product! [...] Promoting the different varieties of English of the Third World with their respective 'national' labels is a major strategy used in the 'language trade'. The English-using citizens of the nations where English is a second language, and the non-resident elites of these nations together are championing their 'national' varieties of English in the name of New Englishes, and the politics of English continues in one form or the other.

> The politics of 'World Englishes' is closely linked with what has been termed as 'cultural colonialism', 'linguistic imperialism', and the building up of new 'empires' in the technological age, using mass media as its major weapon.

> (1998, pp. 10–11)

Krishnaswamy and Burde's point of view here seems to follow Robert Phillipson's (1992) notion of 'linguistic imperialism', according to which the English language is a primary vehicle through which Anglophone Western powers maintain and reinforce their cultural and economic hegemonic positions in the world. This thesis has been criticised by many in the last two decades (see, among others, Bisong, 1995; Davies, 1996; Widdowson, 1998; Holborrow, 1999; Rajagopalan, 1999; Brutt-Griffler, 2002; Wright, 2004; Kirkpatrick, 2007b; Saraceni, 2008). However, Krishnaswamy and Burde's reading of the WE paradigm as a form of linguistic colonialism is interesting for me not so much for its 'linguistic imperialism' colouring as because it suggests quite unequivocally that the geographical and national mapping of world Englishes replicates a view of the world which stems from a European view of the world. In particular, the catalogue of nationally labelled Englishes appears to be based on the nineteenth-century European myth of the nation-state, according to which language, nation and territory are linked by a 'natural' relationship. As seen in Chapter 2, such an idea had an entirely political matrix: "ultimately it is the political ambition of dynasties and power elites which has proved the decisive factor in nation state formation rather than any natural congruence of nation and state" (Wright, 2000, p. 31). If European dynasties established the nation-state fundamentally as a political construct, it seems to me that the identification, classification and denomination of national Englishes in WE academia constitute an *academic* construct, especially if one accepts that "classifications are not objective divisions, inherent in the nature of things, but are structures we impose upon the world" (Collin, 1997, p. 84).

This conceptual problem has been ignored by WE academia. Braj Kachru, for example, has explained that

> [...] the [English] language did 'travel' with the colonizers into regions which had physical realities, with living people, who had names and social, cultural and linguistic identities. The colonies provided locations in which the Raj established its control and implanted the English language.
>
> (2005, p. 216)

This is indeed true: the history and geography of English are undeniable facts. However, this observation overlooks a fundamental point. That English spread into territories inhabited by people with their own names, identities and so on is less than obvious and has to be taken with a great deal of caution. The imperial genesis of most world's countries is a fact that the WE literature tends to understate. English was undoubtedly taken to real places inhabited by real people, but those places and people were deeply transformed in the centuries that followed, and as a result of, that very diaspora. One of the consequences of European (not only British) imperialism was that the map of the world was almost entirely redrawn, countries were created, borders traced, cities given new names and people's identities profoundly undermined, if not completely torn apart. The names and the identities that were in place *before* European imperialism were very, and sometimes unrecognisably, different from those that emerged *during* and *after* it. Thus, the identification, naming and classification of varieties of English in WE literature are based on a world map that has been mostly created by European colonisation and are, at best, a grossly distorted representation of the social, cultural and linguistic groupings of people and their names and at the time of their first 'encounter' with the British and their language. Therefore, although it rejects the idea that England, a European country, should be the norm-providing centre of the English language, the WE paradigm is at the same time trapped in a Eurocentric subdivision of the world, and the superimposition of an imperialist model onto the world map of English seems to be glaringly at odds with the WE egalitarian aim.

Apart from having an inherent inaccurate and contradictory character, the nationally defined nomenclature of world Englishes also contributes to stressing difference among the Englishes it names. This, I contend, distances even further the WE paradigm from the 'club of equals' ideal.

4.4   Equality in difference?

As has been discussed in the previous sections, that the local acculturation of English has given rise to distinct varieties of English is a classic tenet in WE literature and provides the theoretical blueprint for a meticulous categorisation of Englishes. On the basis of this axiom, linguistic differences among Englishes are emphasised and treated seriously, since they are considered reflections of cultural differences. The rigour with which such distinctions are regarded is evinced in the following citation:

> While I use the label "Singaporean English", I am also aware that SE shares many features with Malaysian English (ME) because until relatively recently, Singapore and Malaysia shared a common history under British rule and for a number of years after independence when Singapore was part of Malaysia. The ethnic composition of the speakers in Singapore and the west coast of Peninsular Malaysia also show many similarities. Many accounts therefore consider SE and ME

together [...]. I have therefore found it not inappropriate to use some examples of ME in my discussion below. I also therefore do not consider it problematic that in two of the novels discussed below [...], some of the setting is in present-day Malaysia.

(Tan, 1999, p. 361)

Of course I must stress that it is not my intention to single out one particular author as the unaware victim of something that I consider an epistemological anomaly. My purpose is simply to illustrate the type of concern that is often expressed as a result of it. Here Peter Tan feels the need to justify the use of examples of Malaysian English and of Malaysian settings in his analysis of speech presentation in Singaporean English novels. It seems as if this need may arise from a conviction that referring to Malaysian English in analysing Singaporean English novels trespasses borders which should not normally be trespassed, even though one notices hardly any difference in the use of English when passing the physical border between Malaysia and Singapore. The message however is clear: Malaysian English is not Singaporean English and that is the reason why they are named differently.

The same basic principle applies to all other Englishes. Raja Ram Mehrotra defines Indian English in an orthodox WE manner:

> Indian English (IndE) may broadly be defined as a non-native variety of English used in India. Although based on standard British English (BrE), it has evolved over the years certain linguistic features, distinct from the native variety, in consonance with the socio-cultural and linguistic realities of India. [...] That IndE has come to be established as a viable, vigorous variety has been recognised by scholars both in India and abroad.

(1998, p. 15)

It is evident that the international recognition of Indian English as a "viable" and "vigorous" variety plays a key role in this definition. Mehrotra's conception of Indian English is aligned with that aspiration and is located within the classic WE rubric, whose aim is to eliminate inequality in the perception of peripheral varieties of English by elevating them to the same level of dignity and prestige of Inner-Circle varieties. The evolution and the affirmation of distinct linguistic features are presented here as a necessary condition for the existence of Indian English. They allow Mehrotra to use the acronym IndE alongside BrE, thereby situating Indian English within a catalogue of Englishes that, it is hoped, will have the blessing of the international academic community. In this sense, the use of the acronym IndE is not just a convenient abbreviation: its technical appearance, especially when used in parallel with similar acronyms such as BrE or AmE, is reminiscent of the way elements are included in a chemistry periodic table and is aimed at rendering the categorisation scientific. Thus the scientific proof that all varieties of English are equal is pursued by emphasising their supposedly distinctive linguistic features. This seems to me to be a highly problematic point. Particularly, advocating equality while pointing out and highlighting differences may be counterproductive.

The problem is that the liberal linguist seems to be engaged in a battle whose rules have been set by nationalist linguistics. In a classic sociological study on "Labelling Theory", Becker (1963) stated that

> social groups create deviance by making the rules whose infraction constitutes deviance, and by applying those rules to particular people and labeling them as outsiders. From this point of view, deviance is not a quality of the act the person commits, but rather a consequence of the application by others of rules and sanctions to an "offender." The deviant is one to whom that label has successfully been applied; deviant behavior is behavior that people so label.
>
> (1963, p. 9)

This concept seems to be consonant with WE discourse, where the classic dominant view is that negative labelling has been applied by the purist to non-native varieties of English, which are consequently represented as deviants. However, other forms of labelling operate simultaneously. Above all, the emphasis, in WE literature, on formal linguistic difference reinforces the 'deviant' label affixed onto non-Anglosaxon varieties of English. With reference to the North American context, Becker noted that "[t]he foreign-born and those otherwise ethnically peculiar often have their rules made for them by the Protestant Anglo-Saxon minority" (1963, p. 17). Again, this seems to be applicable in more than one way to the construction of world Englishes:

> The traditional practice of describing New Varieties of English (NVEs) in the Outer Circle with reference to Inner Circle native-speaker norms tends to characterize Outer Circle speakers' usage in wholly negative terms with regard to their general proficiency level, the credibility of their intuitive judgements, and their overall authority over the language in terms of their confidence and sophistication in

the use of English. This is because most descriptions of these varieties have tended to use difference as a means of defining them.

(Rubdy et al., 2008, p. 46)

The use of difference as a defining factor is the primary rule in the purist's game. Language purists reject the validity of so-called non-standard varieties because they generally consider variation a form of degradation of language and cite examples of particularly 'deviant' grammatical, lexical or phonological items in order to corroborate their arguments against what they see as the uncontrolled alteration of linguistic rules. By apparent contrast, WE scholars regard variation as an integral part of the continuous evolution of language in different societies and posit that 'new' varieties of English should be treated as valid as the 'old' ones. In pursuing this goal, they, like language purists, focus their attention on what they regard as non-standard forms and cite the same 'deviant' features as examples of the acculturation of English. WE scholars focus on difference and deviation just as much as language purists do. The traditional practice mentioned by Rubdy et al. of defining 'new' varieties of English in terms of the degree to which they deviate from 'old' ones is not challenged or abandoned but embraced in WE discourse. Indeed, the very idea of distinct Englishes entails the presence of a reference point acting as a benchmark, against which certain features are foregrounded and identified as distinctive. In this way, world Englishes are inescapably located in a subaltern position with respect to Anglo-American English, a position of constant comparison with the norm-providing Inner Circle. The idea that 'non-native' varieties of English may be normatively autonomous from 'native' varieties is illusory if the two are placed in an inextricable relationship whereby the former are defined by their being different from the latter. Within this model, 'non-native' varieties of English *need* 'native' varieties in order to characterise their distinctiveness and, hence, their very existence. Non-Inner-Circle varieties of English are described according to parameters that have been set *in* the Inner Circle, *for* the Inner Circle and *by* the Inner Circle.

The philosophy of one best, monolithic and Anglosaxon English is based on imperialist-like ideology which makes use of precarious language descriptions in order to provide evidence for its assertions. The weakest point in the WE paradigm is the will to challenge those assertions by validating the flawed language descriptions on which they are based. Responding to the claim that Indian English is incomprehensible by striving to demonstrate that it does not miss a chance to discredit that claim more effectively at its root. Crucially, the very expression of hope that the legitimacy of varieties of Englishes could be shown through empirical and rigorous investigation indirectly lends credibility to the claim that such varieties may actually be inferior.

The fallacy is in the objectification of language. The inaccuracy in the claim that Indian English is incomprehensible is not so much about the degree of comprehensibility of Indian English as about the notion that there is an object that should be called 'Indian English', different from another object that should be called 'British English', and that both objects can be shown to be linguistically distinct. In this regard, it is significant that, just a few lines below his definition of Indian English, Mehrotra goes on to emphasise its international prominence by referring to the literary achievements of Arundhati Roy:

> That Arundhati Roy has won the 1997 Booker Prize, Britain's most prestigious literary award, for her first novel *The God of Small Things*, in spite of political compulsions and ideological considerations which generally influence such awards, speaks volumes of the immense potential role that IndE can play in portraying and projecting Indian life and milieu to the world.
>
> (1998, pp. 15–16)

This assumes that

- there is an 'Indian English' that can be identified with precision as a distinct variety of English;
- being Indian, Arundathy Roy is a user of Indian English;
- she wrote *The God of Small Things* in Indian English.

Mehrotra, therefore, seems to ascribe much of the merit for the award of the 1997 Prize to "the immense potential role" that Indian English plays in "portraying and projecting Indian life and milieu". Indeed, if one follows his reasoning to the letter, it would appear that it was Indian English, not so much Arundhati Roy, that won the literary award, and since the existence of Indian English is based on identifiable distinct linguistic features, one could conclude that the 1997 Booker Prize was won thanks to the intrinsic quality, the vigour perhaps, of the lexis, the grammar, the syntax, the thematic structure, the cohesive patterns and so on of Indian English. This extremely reductive interpretation constitutes an example of the objectification of language pushed to the extreme.

Indeed, even if the description of Indian English as 'viable' and 'vigorous' is aimed at legitimising this variety of English, it actually ends up legitimising the linguistically wholly unsound claim that a language *can* be considered viable, not viable, vigorous, weak and so on. Ultimately, it fuels and legitimises precisely the perception of inequality among languages and varieties and of the nations associated with them. As McColl Millar underlines,

> In theory, all varieties of language are equal. In essence, all human beings have the same ability to communicate all ideas, both abstract and concrete. Yet this is not our perception of the way the (linguistic) world works. We all assume that some varieties of language, more importantly, that some languages, possess greater economic and political resources than do others. The source of these inequalities is power: political, economic, cultural, historical and social power. This power can often be expressed in terms of national prestige.
>
> (McColl Millar, 2005, p. 199)

4.5   A club of equals or an exclusive club?

A quality scale of Englishes can be construed precisely on the basis of the conceptualisation and classification of world Englishes. By highlighting difference and foregrounding distinction, these categorising structures may play a decisive role in creating in this context something very similar to Link and Phelan's concept of stigma:

> [S]tigma exists when the following interrelated components converge. In the first component, people distinguish and label human differences. In the second, dominant cultural beliefs link labeled persons to undesirable characteristics – to negative stereotypes. In the third, labeled persons are placed in distinct categories so as to accomplish some degree of separation of "us" from "them." In the fourth, labeled persons experience status loss and discrimination that lead to unequal outcomes. Finally, stigmatization is entirely contingent on access to social, economic, and political power that allows the identification of differentness, the construction of stereotypes, the separation of labeled persons into distinct categories, and the full execution of disapproval, rejection, exclusion, and discrimination.
>
> (Link and Phelan, 2001, p. 367)

The labelling of varieties of English facilitates the attachment of undesirable characteristics to them, with the result that such labelled Englishes are segregated and marginalised. As I mentioned earlier, varieties of English tend to be objectified and treated as separate items on the basis of certain distinctive features that are subjectively singled out. The problem is that

> once differences are identified and labeled, they are typically taken for granted as being just the way things are [even though] substantial oversimplification is required to create groups [...] when there is enormous variability within the resulting categories and no clear demarcation between categories on almost any criterion one can think of.
>
> (Link and Phelan, 2001, p. 367)

The enormous variability that exists within each named variety of English signals the oversimplification of the categorisation involved and the artificiality of nationally defined premodifiers. Instead of reflecting objective attributes of the varieties they designate, each one of such premodifiers acts as a label, that is, "something that is affixed" and therefore "leaves the validity of the designation an open question" (2001, p. 368). In addition, apart from being identified with dubious accuracy, the items denominated by means of labels can also undergo a process of discrimination, since when they are "set apart, and linked to undesirable characteristics, a rationale is constructed for devaluing, rejecting, and excluding them" (2001, p. 371).

For Outer-Circle 'varieties' of English, the 'undesirable characteristics' are precisely those 'features' that set them apart from those 'varieties' commonly held as 'standard'. The result of such a strategy is likely to be the irremediable and perpetual stigmatisation of the 'object' Indian English, associated to such trivial 'facts' as 'I am knowing', or the object 'Malaysian English', associated to 'lah', etc. At best, these forms have become popularised as quaint features of equally quaint Englishes, oddities to be observed with interest and amusement, even catalogued perhaps, in a sort of quasi-zoological fashion, each one in its own cage furnished with an information plate bearing its scientific name. At worst, they are seen as evidence of the outright unacceptability of varieties of English outside the Anglosaxon circle, thus reinforcing, with complete faithfulness, the purist's stance.

4.6 Conclusion

In this chapter I have argued that the articulation of the egalitarian ideological position in the WE paradigm has been built on foundations
made rather insecure by

- the inability of the semiotics of the model to represent the complex
  and multi-layered meanings it intends to encode;
- its replication of a theoretically flawed and ideologically Eurocentric
  conceptualisation of language;
- its susceptibility to interpretations which can be in polar opposition
  to those very meanings, such as the possibility that all Englishes
  outside the 'Inner Circle' may be stigmatised as deviant and inappropriate.

The argument that I have tried to make is that the WE paradigm does
not really distance itself from an epistemological system in which the
First World describes the Third World in the First World's own terms and,
inevitably, as a corrupted, deviant, imperfect, deficient and inferior version of the First World. Thus, non-Anglosaxon Englishes are otherised,
in Edward Said's (1978) sense of the term: Nigerian English, Indian
English, Malaysian English and so on are 'oriental' forms of English,
opposed to the occidental ones, which are the exclusive occupiers of the
deictic centre in the relationship between the two. Meanwhile, modifiers
such as *Nigerian, Indian, Malaysian* and so on suggest that the varieties
thus denominated are significantly different from English proper and
from 'proper' English, which can remain comfortably synonymous to
British or *American*.

5
English as a Lingua Franca

> when our hearts have become one,
> … we shall reach a common language
> with a common script, whilst we shall retain
> provincial languages for provincial use.
>
> —Gandhi

5.1 Introduction

As was seen in Chapters 3 and 4, the WE paradigm is concerned with the ways in which English, the former imperial language, has been appropriated and reforged locally in different parts of the world, giving rise to a myriad of Englishes, all distinctive in form but equal in value and dignity. Fundamentally, the WE school of thought seeks to decentralise and pluralise the concept 'English' and to provide representations of it alternative to the Anglocentric model. Accordingly, WE literature has repeatedly criticised purist positions about English, the argument being that English is not just a British or American language but also an Indian, Ghanaian, Malaysian and so on language. Learners and users of English around the world need not be dependent on exonormative models but should be able to rely on endonormative ones.

While WE scholars' efforts have focussed on the 'Outer Circle', a number of researches have in recent years begun to turn their attention to the 'Expanding Circle', that is, to those parts of the world where English does not have a postcolonial presence but is used primarily as an international lingua franca (e.g. Jenkins, 2000, 2006a, 2007, 2009; Seidlhofer, 2001, 2006, 2009; Cogo and Dewey, 2006; Kirkpatrick, 2006; Dewey, 2007).

As Barbara Seidlhofer states, "the term 'English as a lingua franca' (ELF) has emerged as a way of referring to communication in English between speakers with different first languages" (2005, p. 339). Thus, English may be used as a lingua franca in the European Parliament, among university exchange students, by tourists and travellers, in international business meetings and in countless other contexts. ELF scholars maintain that a better understanding and extensive description of how these interactions look and sound like can lead to a recognition of their functional validity and to a consequent abandonment of the deep-rooted deficit view of 'Expanding-Circle' or 'non-native' English. This enhanced description and understanding of ELF is to be pursued through the construction of corpora of speakers' use of ELF, so that large amounts of data can then be reliably described. Within this line of reasoning, the achievement of this objective can in turn empower learners and users of English and remove the pressure of having to constantly look to 'native-speaker English' as the only repository of linguistic truth.

In this sense, academics interested in ELF share the same aims as those interested in world Englishes:

> WE and ELF are similar in that they have four common working axioms: emphasizing the pluricentricity of English, seeking variety recognition, accepting that language changes and adapts itself to new environments, and highlighting the discourse strategies of English-knowing bilinguals.
>
> (Pakir, 2009, p. 228)

The relatively new ELF research field is still very much establishing its parameters, scope and goals, and this protracted phase of development has benefited from the criticism, sometimes harsh, dismissive, or sceptical, from other applied linguists who often share the same general aims. I have participated in this criticism myself and, in reiterating some of the main points already made elsewhere (Rubdy and Saraceni, 2006; Saraceni, 2008), in this chapter I nonetheless argue that the notion of ELF may actually contain the seeds of a radical change in the conceptualisation of the English language.

5.2   Tracing the steps of ELF

Towards the beginning of the new millennium, the WE model's exclusive focus on the 'Outer Circle' began to feel somewhat restrictive, as the presence and use of English became more firmly established, and recognised as a lingua franca, in the Expanding Circle. Thus, while the preoccupations of WE scholars were seen as relevant to settings where different varieties of English were used intranationally, some researchers began to see the necessity to devote their attention to contexts where English was mainly used as an international language. The main source of inspiration for the development of this area of academic enquiry can be said to have come to a large extent form Jennifer Jenkins' work on the phonology of English as an international language (2000). Based on the classification and the description of core and non-core features of phonology among speakers of English worldwide, Jenkins demonstrated how it was not necessary to spend time and energy in teaching and learning all aspects of phonology in an attempt to emulate models that were misleadingly construed as 'native-like' and how it was instead advisable to concentrate one's attention on those features which cause actual problems of intelligibility. This principle was later expanded to lexicogrammar and incorporated in what came to be known as ELF research, whose aim was that of providing a comprehensive and empirical account of English as a lingua franca.

In a programmatic paper, Barbara Seidlhofer (2001) identified a "conceptual gap" and sought to attend to it by first of all pointing out that Outer-Circle national Englishes were not necessarily suitable for the Expanding Circle. The central idea was that since in the Expanding Circle English is used primarily as an international lingua franca rather than as a national language, the only feasible way for users of English therein to not have to depend on ENL norms would be to make available a model that would be alternative not only to ENL but also to postcolonial varieties of English, which were neither sociopolitically nor culturally relevant in the rest of the world. From this point of view, the description of ELF was seen as instrumental in the quest for a de-nationalised model of English for the Expanding Circle that would complete the range of options available to learners and users of English around the world. In order to achieve this objective, ELF needed to be described in the same way as national Englishes had been. This was seen as important especially because although many sociolinguistic studies had focussed their attention upon the features of postcolonial varieties of English, none had attempted to document the features of ELF.

ELF researchers, thus, see their project as complementing and expanding on WE research. In her 'conceptual gap' paper, Seidlhofer considered it a task of ELF research "to build on the pioneering work which has been done on indigenized varieties of English" (2001, p. 150). In this respect, she cited Ayo Bamgboṣe' call for a codification of the endonormative standards of 'non-native Englishes' (1998) as a necessary step towards their full recognition and stated that the same aim should be pursued in 'Expanding-Circle' contexts. This was particularly important in English language pedagogy, where native-speaker models still played a major role, despite a greater sociolinguistic and cultural awareness about the diversity of English and significant advancements in teaching methodology:

> Changes in the perception of the role of English in the world have significantly influenced current thinking about approaches to teaching (if not necessarily the teaching itself) and led to an increased socio-political and intercultural awareness [...]. However, as far as linguistic models as targets for learning are concerned, these usually do not figure as a focal concern, or matter for reflection, at all, and so, whether explicitly or implicitly, native-speaker models have largely remained unquestioned. This means that the *how* is changing, but linked to a *what* that is not. Certainly no linguistically radical proposals have been put forward which would match the thrust of the important innovations which have taken place in pedagogy. In short, no coherent and comprehensive lingua franca model has been proposed so far which does justice to these changes in terms of the actual language taught.
>
> (Seidlhofer, 2001, p. 140)

The idea was that a new *what*, that is, a "coherent and comprehensive lingua franca model" should replace 'native-speaker' models and it was precisely for this reason that Seidlhofer felt it was necessary to "profile ELF as a viable variety" (2001, p. 144) and "explore the possibility of a codification of ELF with a conceivable ultimate objective of making it a feasible, acceptable and respected alternative to ENL in appropriate contexts of use" (2001, p. 150).

On the surface, the intentions of the ELF project seem not only wholly reasonable but also desirable. However, liberating and sensible as it may appear to be, if the almost commonsensical soundness of this proposal is probed a little deeper, some important conceptual and practical problems emerge.

5.3   Reshaping the conceptual gap

Fundamentally, the move from the non-necessity to worry about non-core aspects of pronunciation to the necessity to know certain significantly frequent and intelligible features of English entailed a didactic proposition:

> [...] anyone participating in international communication needs to be familiar with, and have in their linguistic repertoire for use, as and when appropriate, certain forms (phonological, lexicogrammatical, etc.) that are widely used and widely intelligible across groups of English speakers from different first language backgrounds.
>
> (Jenkins, 2006b, p. 161)

One immediate question comes to mind, namely, it appears that the ELF project wants to make available another exonormative model alongside existing ones. Even assuming that an ELF model can actually be described and codified, it is difficult to imagine how exactly it would differ from ENL in terms of its being located *externally* to its users. In other words, it is not clear how a model of English devised by researchers through rigorous description of extensive data can really be more relevant and *closer* to ELF users than, say, models based on 'British English' or 'American English'. Bamgboṣe's idea of codification refers to uses of English that, within a WE rubric at least, have become endonormatively standardised within particular settings, such as, for example, Nigeria. If the same concept is applied to ELF, the necessary assumption is that billions of ELF speakers use English in a sufficiently uniform way as to warrant the possibility that ELF may indeed be a codifiable variety. But, given the scale of ELF use worldwide, this would appear to be a hazardous hypothesis.

The development of an ELF model would presumably involve a process of substantial synthesis. It is for this reason that one of the criticisms that have stimulated particularly vigorous and useful responses from ELF researchers is the perception that they seemed to want to promote a model of English which would be artificially reductionist and hence "different from all the real encounters available to [learners] outside the classroom" (Rubdy and Saraceni, 2006, p. 11), thereby disregarding the "polymorphous nature of the English language worldwide" (p. 13). Advantageously, this has induced ELF researchers to begin to clarify that this was not the case. In the same volume where it was made, Seidlhofer called this criticism "a misconception" (2006, p. 40). Elsewhere, Jenkins defined it a "misplaced criticism" (2006b, p. 162), a "misrepresentation of ELF researchers" (2007, p. 19) and a "strange interpretation of ELF" (2009, p. 202).

The "effort to set the record straight" (Jenkins, 2007, p. 19) has indeed been admirable. Even though the direct responses to our perplexities have been characterised by *negative* definitions, in that they have focussed more on elucidating what ELF is *not* than on explaining what it is, undoubtedly there has been an evident evolution and development of ideas in ELF literature, precisely concerning the very 'object' under scrutiny. In particular, questions are being raised as to

- whether or not ELF refers to a set of common linguistic features shared by its users;
- whether such 'common ground' is shared universally or, perhaps, it is significantly defined by regional character;
- whether the study of ELF should be concerned with linguistic features at all or it should instead shift its focus towards strategies of meaning negotiation and ownership of the language.

Those are extremely important points, the resolution of which is not only essential within ELF research but also central to a more general reconceptualisation of English in the world. The nodal question is: what is ELF?

5.4   What is ELF?

In a recent monograph Jennifer Jenkins lamented that "scholars who recognize the legitimacy of ELF are at present in a fairly small minority among linguists (even, surprisingly, sociolinguistics [*sic*] and applied linguists)" (2007, p. 7). She goes as far as to argue that "scholarly opposition to ELF seems to be based not so much on rational argument as on irrational prejudice" (2007, p. 12). Jenkins seems puzzled by the fact that while "ELF is seen as non-controversial and is taken for granted by many professionals working internationally (businesspeople, technicians, and suchlike) [...] negative responses to ELF [come] primarily from within the field of English studies" (2009, p. 202). It seems to me, however, that ELF is not at all controversial. That English is the most important lingua franca in the world may have different connotations and implications for different people but is nonetheless an undisputed fact. Also, since the work of sociolinguists and applied linguists in general is not typically driven by irrationally conservative sentiments, it is quite possible that all the misconceptions and negative responses that have supposedly been expressed towards ELF might be the result of a certain degree of confusion in the ways in which ELF has been postulated.

The first source of confusion lies in the characterisation of ELF as a variety of English. Jenkins defines it as "an emerging English that exists in its *own right* and which is being described in its *own terms*" (2007, p. 2), suggesting that it is one of the many varieties of English in the world. This particular emerging English is also broken down into different varieties: "ELF varieties are used internationally rather than intranationally" (2007, p. 17), and "it is entirely for learners to decide what kind of English they want to learn, be it EFL [...] an ESL (outer circle) variety, or an ELF variety for international communication (for example, China English, Spanish English, Japanese English, etc.)" (2007, pp. 21–22). So ELF appears to be one variety, possibly with its own features, or a set of nationally defined varieties, presumably characterised by their own peculiar linguistic features, in much the same way as world Englishes are generally thought of.

Seidlhofer, by contrast, is much more cautious in this regard:

> Whether ELF should be called a variety of English at all is an open question, and one which cannot be answered as long as we do not have any good descriptions of it. [...]. Once descriptions are available of how speakers from different linguacultural backgrounds use ELF, this will make it possible to consider whether it would make sense to think of English as it is spoken by its non-native speakers as falling into different varieties, just as is the English spoken by its native speakers.
>
> (2006, p. 46)

Here Seidlhofer stresses the importance of rigorous descriptions of ELF in order to establish in what ways ELF fits with the concept of variety. However, as Saraceni (2008) and Berns (2009) have pointed out, the very idea that ELF *may* be a variety, or a set of varieties, is part of a more profound confusion as to whether the term ELF is used to denote a particular *form* of English or a particular *function* of it:

> [ELF] research [...] is based upon the assumption that "lingua franca" is the appropriate label not only for a sociolinguistic function of a language – i.e. its use as a tool for interpersonal communication among speakers with no single language in common – but also for the system of the forms that are peculiar to a specific variety of a language.
>
> (Berns, 2009, p. 192)

The problem is that what ELF *does* is made to coincide to what it *is*. Andy Kirkpatrick, for example, laments the scarcity of "analysis and descriptions" of ELF "despite this extremely widespread and common *function* of English" (2007a, p. 155, my emphasis). Analogously, according to Seidlhofer, ELF is "a way of referring to communication in English between speakers with different first languages" (2005, p. 339) and it is necessary to study systematically "what it looks and sounds like and how people actually use it and make it work" (pp. 339–340). This entails that communication in English between speakers with different first languages has its own 'look' and 'sound'. More precisely, since the definition above "does not preclude the participation of English native speakers in ELF interaction" (p. 339), the assumption is that if an instance of communication in English includes people who somehow do not qualify as 'English native speakers', the English used therein will have a distinctive lexical, grammatical and/or phonological form. This correlation can be represented with the following formula:

$$if\,(\exists s \in S : s = NNS, ELF, ENL)$$

where s is any speaker and S is a group of speakers participating in an instance of communication. The formula says that if there is at least one speaker who is a 'non-native speaker' of English then the language is ELF, otherwise it is ENL. The formula represents the axiom that the *form* ELF follows the *function* ELF, which is a core tenet in ELF research, as explained by Cogo:

> ELF users from different first language backgrounds orient to communicative success. Research has shown that on a practical level, speakers of ELF are less concerned about adhering to native speaker standards and more concerned about their communicative skills. [...] In these situations and communities, ELF is both form *and* function; besides, by performing certain functions it is appropriated by its speakers and changed in form. In other words, form seems to follow function and start a circular phenomenon of variation and change.
>
> (2008, p. 60)

That ELF speakers are less concerned with 'native speaker' norms than they are with effective communication may be true, but the fundamental point to make here is that the non-adherence to someone else's standards does not in any way entail the presence of an alternative standard shared by ELF speakers. In other words, it is impossible to postulate the existence of Y simply by stating that it is not X. If ELF is *not* ENL, we still have no idea what it *is*:

> [...] acceptance of the very concept of ELF as a legitimate alternative to the concept of ENL will be furthered when it is clearer *just what it is* that is waiting to be accepted – that is, when documentation and analyses of a wide range of speech events carried out through ELF become available.
>
> (Seidlhofer, 2009, p. 239, my emphasis)

The question remains unanswered after the necessity was first identified for "an investigation of what (if anything), notwithstanding all the diversity, might emerge as common features of ELF use, irrespective of speakers' first languages and levels of proficiency" (Seidlhofer, 2001, p. 147). Seidlhofer is bewildered by the insufficiency of formal description of ELF and attributes it to widespread reluctance to accept it as a legitimate 'object of investigation':

> [...] currently, there is a very considerable gap between the extent of the spread of ELF and the extent to which efforts have been made to describe it. This lag is likely to be due to [...] the difficulty that seems to be inherent in accepting a language that is not anybody's native tongue as a legitimate object of investigation and descriptive research.
>
> (Seidlhofer, 2009, p. 237)

However, the problem lies, in my opinion, in the very characterisation of ELF as *object* and in the unavoidable ineffability of it intended as a set of 'common features'. The presence of speakers of different first languages in an instance of communication may well be a variable contributing to the shape of the language used in that particular instance, but to hypothesise that that single variable may actually determine a distinctive type of English common to all other instances of communication involving second-language speakers is unrealistic, to say the least. Form does indeed follow function, yet not in the sense intended here, but in a completely opposite sense. This is explained quite clearly by Berns, who, for illustrative purposes, refers to two meetings among European speakers as real examples of ELF interaction and remarks that transcripts of the two meetings would not actually show anything about English as a lingua franca:

> Rather, what they would show is how each particular group came to terms with negotiating meaning in a particular situation for a

particular audience and with a particular goal in mind. The formal features these negotiations take would reflect each of these elements, and might or might not reoccur with other configurations of participants, of situation, of audience, of goal.

(Berns, 2009, p. 197)

Form follows function, and does so in each individual instance of communication. Hence, " 'lingua franca' is an abstraction, a concept; it is not a language (or variety) *per se*" (Berns, 2009, p. 196). It is for this reason that it is impossible to describe it as an abstraction:

Because of the diversity at the heart of this communicative medium, LFE [(Lingua Franca English)] is intersubjectively constructed in each specific context of interaction. The form of this English is negotiated by each set of speakers for their purposes. The speakers are able to monitor each other's language proficiency to determine mutually the appropriate grammar, phonology, lexical range, and pragmatic conventions that would ensure intelligibility. Therefore, it is difficult to describe this language a priori.

(Canagarajah, 2007, p. 925)

In the face of these reflections, it is not surprising that definitions of ELF have been so widely different and that "the acronym is used as an umbrella to shelter multiple meanings and pragmatic intentions, not all of them consistent with each other" (Prodromou, 2007, p. 48). Here is a sample:

Table 5.1   Definitions of ELF

A way of referring to communication in English between speakers with different first languages	*A form of communication* (Seidlhofer, 2005, p. 339)
A medium of communication [used] by people who do not speak the same first language	*A medium of communication* (Kirkpatrick, 2007a, p. 155)
An emerging English that exists in its *own right* and which is being described in its *own terms*	*A variety of English* (Jenkins, 2007, p. 2)
An umbrella term that encompasses all types of communication among bilingual users of English in the Expanding Circle but allows for local realisations as well as extensive use of accommodation strategies and code-switching	*An all-encompassing term* (Cogo, 2008, p. 58)
The worldwide employment of the English language as a means of communication	*English in the world* (House, 2009, p. 141)

The incongruity among these definitions is symptomatic of a field in continuous evolution. While there continues to be an interest in the description of the formal linguistic features of ELF and data continue to be collected, such interest is expressed with a greater degree of caution and tentativeness. As Jenkins admits,

> At present there is insufficient evidence for researchers to be able to predict the extent of the common ELF ground. And it is also likely that researchers working on ELF in different parts of the world [...] will identify different branches of ELF [...] and different sub-varieties within these. But at present it is still too early to say.
>
> (Jenkins, 2009, p. 201)

Kirkpatrick's work on ELF in the Association of South East Asian Nations (ASEAN) region (Deterding and Kirkpatrick, 2006; Kirkpatrick, 2008) is an example of the localisation of ELF research. However, what is much more significant and interesting is that a shift of focus is taking place from the phonological and lexicogrammatical features of ELF to the pragmatic strategies of meaning negotiations in ELF interactions that both Berns and Canagarajah refer to. The interest on the code is not abandoned, but it seems to be sidelined by a renewed interest on language behaviour.

5.5   A shift of focus in ELF research

As Jenkins clarifies, "ELF researchers are as interested in the kinds of linguistic processes involved in ELF creativity as they are in the resulting surface-level features" (Jenkins, 2009, p. 201). Seidlhofer is even more explicit: "it is an understanding of the more general communicative *processes* that is the main objective of documenting and observing *how* ELF speakers interact" (Seidlhofer, 2009, p. 240, my emphasis). The focus on processes of communication and on 'how' they unfold constitutes an important shift of perspective from the one which concentrated on the 'what' (see the citation from Seidlhofer (2001) on page 85). Especially, the idea of proposing a comprehensive lingua franca model seems to have been surpassed, and the description of formal linguistic features is seen as a means rather than an end:

> Rather than limiting itself to the identification of particular linguistic features, this research has tended to take a much more processual, communicative view of ELF, of which linguistic features constitute

but a part and are investigated not for their own sake but as indications of the various functions ELF fulfils in the interactions observed. So the crucial challenge has been to move from the surface description of particular features, however interesting they may be in themselves, to an explanation of the underlying significance of the forms: to ask what work they do, what functions they are symptomatic of. And the explanations that are found when analysing the accomplished interactional work that speakers undertake via ELF very often have to do with 'behavioural norms', with pragmatic and creative processes.

(Seidlhofer, 2009, p. 241)

Within this re-orientation, there begins to be explicit recognition that "[i]t is perhaps helpful to see lingua franca more as a *functional* term rather than a *linguistic* one" (Kirkpatrick, 2008, p. 28) and that "[i]t is [...] neither possible nor desirable to attempt a description of a uniform ELF variety – this cannot be appropriate given the variability of lingua franca communication" (Dewey, 2007, p. 349). Indeed, even the possibility that a description of ELF could somehow provide a pedagogic model seems to have become less attractive:

> [...] if and when ELF features have been definitively identified and perhaps eventually codified. ELF researchers do not claim that these features should necessarily be taught to English learners. In other words, they do not believe either that pedagogic decisions about language teaching should follow on automatically from language descriptions or that the linguists compiling the corpora should make those decisions.

(Jenkins, 2009, p. 202)

In acknowledging this paradigm shift in ELF research, Martin Dewey makes a case for situating the findings of such research within broader issues of globalisation. Drawing from the transformationalist perspective on globalisation theorised by various scholars (e.g. Giddens, 2002), Dewey argues that "ELF interactions [...] are epitomical of the role of local appropriation in globalization" (2007, p. 349). In other words, he sees ELF communication as the locus where active, effective and conscious reformulation of the norms of English obtain, and something which the ELT establishment should acknowledge and come to terms with. From this point of view, the appropriation of English that is taking place in ELF communication is not dissimilar from that which, according to the WE literature, has taken place in postcolonial settings. Dewey sees ELF as reflecting the fundamentally dynamic and fluid nature of language and of the continued diversification that results from it:

> As language practitioners we must acknowledge the pluralism involved in language use, otherwise we face the risk of continually freezing English spatially and temporally. Unerring adherence to an essentially monolithic concept of language is counter to the diversification of English globally. By subscribing to a transformationalist view of globalization we are better able to move forward from conventional notions of language, variety and speech community. We are thus better able to comprehend, theorize and incorporate in practice the current heightened diversification of English.
>
> (Dewey, 2007, p. 348)

I completely agree with the statement above. Understanding language diversification and informing pedagogic practice with it are eminently necessary. Accordingly, attempts to 'freeze' language are counterproductive to that aim. The problem with the ELF research rubric is that codification still features quite prominently and is "recognized as a crucial requirement", even though it "needs to be modulated according to the different sociohistorical conditions of the Expanding Circle" (Seidlhofer, 2009, p. 240). Even if 'modulated', codification is, by definition, a way of fixing language forms and making them somehow official. And here, therefore, lies the contradiction between the perceived necessity to codify ELF and the recognised unsoundness of attempting to freeze English.

Dewey (2007, p. 348) cites Joseph (2006), who highlights the danger of codifying world Englishes and disregarding their fluid state. As Dewey points out, Joseph is of the opinion that world Englishes are best thought of as an attitude rather than linguistic systems. However, Dewey claims that "there also comes a time when systematizing must take place if this 'attitude' is to become a completely meaningful one" (2007, p. 348). This I find a rather puzzling statement. The difference between attitude and system is absolutely cardinal here. If our attitude to English, and indeed to language in general, is one which regards diversification not as an inevitable by-product of geographical spread but as pertaining to the very nature of language, then trying to codify (or systematise) instances of diversification, no matter how many we choose to take into account, would be a flawed exercise because of two reasons:

1. it would provide a static representation of something which is inherently dynamic;
2. it could only be based on arbitrary, preconceived parameters of norms and deviations thereof.

The second point merits further elaboration. Among the 'features' of ELF that are apparently emerging in the data is a more flexible use of the definite article *the*. Dewey cites samples of conversations where the use of *the* does not adhere to ENL norms. In particular, there are cases where *the* is used with nouns with generic references (e.g. 'the nature', 'the society' and 'the abortion') and cases where speakers do not use the definite article in cases where it would normally be used in ENL. He considers these instances indications of "a shift away from a distinction between specific and generic reference" in ELF, where "[i]f an item is deemed particularly important it is often preceded by the definite article, while if the item is relatively unimportant the zero article is often used" (Dewey, 2007, p. 341). More generally, for Dewey "what is important here is the illustrative value of these cases of linguistic innovation to demonstrate the flexible nature of English" and this confirms that "language [...] is best seen as a dynamic set of non-determinable resources which can be manipulated by its innumerous speakers to suit the many varied communicative purposes it fulfills" (p. 341).

If language is to be understood in this way, a view to which I entirely subscribe, there are two issues here. The first one has to do with the interpretation of data and the false distinction between 'error' and 'difference'. The second regards the treatment of ELF speakers as a special category of English users.

5.5.1   Error or difference?

I think we need to be extremely careful with the interpretation of available data, especially when their quantity is admittedly not as large as one would hope. I am very reluctant to accept that the use of *the* mentioned above is an example of linguistic innovation, fascinating as this hypothesis would be. This is because we cannot ignore that there are languages (e.g. Romance languages such as Italian and French) where the definite article is used much more often than in English, and others (e.g. Slavonic languages such as Polish and Russian or East Asian languages such as Thai or Japanese) that do not even have articles. It is very common for Italian learners of English to use the definite article with general nouns like *society* or *nature*, as this is the norm in Italian.

Conversely, it is equally typical of, say, Polish learners to omit articles or to be unsure when or why to use them. I do not think these are instances of linguistic innovation. Indeed, *innovation* here can be a polished, alternative term to the more negative-sounding *error*, as both terms highlight usages that are marked for their departure from norms considered 'standard' or 'correct' by the external observer/researcher. Indeed, the ELF ethos seems to be caught in the distinction between 'error' and 'difference':

> [...] ELF distinguishes between *difference* (i.e. from ENL) and *deficiency* (i.e. interlanguage or 'learner language'), and does not assume that an item that differs from ENL is by definition an error. It may instead be a legitimate ELF variant. This does not mean, however, that all ELF speakers are proficient: they can also be learners of ELF or not fully competent *non*-learners, making errors just like learners of any second language [...]. At present it is still to some extent an empirical question as to which items are ELF variants and which ELF errors, and depends on factors such as systematicity, frequency, and communicative effectiveness.
>
> (Jenkins, 2009, p. 202)

It is clear that the distinction is only nominal. Within this optic, ENL, whatever it may refer to, represents the frame of reference from which ELF speakers are likely to depart. The likelihood for ELF speakers to disobey ENL norms, whichever these may be, is apparently linked to the range of possible types of English users they can be, and how pervasive their status of 'not fully proficient speaker' is:

Not fully proficient	Learners
	Non-learners
Proficient	Non-learners

Of course there are immediate questions to be asked. What and who determines the degree of proficiency of ELF speakers? How does a 'not fully proficient' speaker become fully proficient? Since 'difference' is measured against ENL norms, the status of 'fully proficient speaker of English' will presumably depend on one's capacity to adhere to such norms. However, some departures from them will be deemed erroneous, others legitimate variants. Again, who makes this judgement? Systematicity and frequency can be calculated with the help of corpus analysis, but why should they say anything about the (non-)error status of a particular expression? This seems to be based on a view of language as a highly regulated system, in which items are (un-)acceptable on the basis of their being *normal*. But how is this measure of *normal*ity connected to effective communication? Is it not up to the participants in any instance of communication to decide if and to what extent language is being used effectively and to act accordingly? Is it not up to them to select and, if necessary, manipulate the non-determinable dynamic resources of a language?

Emphasis on formal linguistic features leads to speculative conclusions which are not useful if we are serious about reconceptualising language as something other than a frozen monolith.

5.5.2   ELF speakers as a special category

The second point to make with regard to a possible reconceptualisation of language within an ELF rubric is that it seems odd to isolate ELF speakers as being especially prone to making efficient use of linguistic resources according to their communicative purposes. Surely this is something *all* language users do. Could this not correspond to a definition of language use? Indeed, Cogo's umbrella-term definition of ELF and House's (p. 91) seem to point in this direction. These definitions are so vast that they can be applied to language communication in general, as it normally takes place in the world, whether or not it involves English. However, one gets the impression that ELF scholars treat lingua franca communicative situations as somewhat peculiarly special. Referring to ELF users, Seidlhofer states that

> ELF users [...] exploit the potential of the language, they are fully involved in the interactions, whether for work or for play. They are focused on the purpose of the talk and on their interlocutors as people, and emphatically not on the linguistic code itself. We can observe people absorbed in the ad hoc, situated negotiation of meaning – an entirely pragmatic undertaking in that the focus is on establishing the indexical link between the code and the context. [...] the interactants are making use of their multi-faceted multilingual repertoires in a fashion motivated by the communicative purpose and the interpersonal dynamics of the interaction.
>
> (2009, p. 242)

Similarly, Jenkins offers advice on how we should behave in ELF contexts:

> [...] from an ELF perspective we all need to make adjustments to our local English variety for the benefit of our interlocutors when we take part in lingua franca English communication. ELF is thus a question, not of orientation to the norms of a particular group of English speakers, but of mutual negotiation involving efforts and adjustments from all parties.
>
> (Jenkins, 2009, p. 201)

The linguistic behaviour described by Seidlhofer and Jenkins above is certainly not restricted to ELF situations, and it is singular that ELF researchers seem to believe that it is. Within a worldwide context, most people in the world are bi- or multilingual, use different linguistic varieties and registers, mix languages and switch between them according to a range of contextual factors. Indeed, in a Firthian sense, it is the context of situation that will determine how individual language users select and/or manipulate linguistic items in order to suit their contextually determined needs.

5.6 Conclusion

Ultimately, I think that ELF communication needs not be treated in any special way. 'English as a Lingua franca' is after all a term which refers rather loosely to the role that English plays when it is "used as the language of communication among people with no language other than English in common" (Berns, 2009, personal communication). This role need not involve distinctions between 'first' and 'second' languages. As it is typical for most people's linguistic repertoire to include more than one language, most human communication will involve, to some degree, the use of a 'lingua franca'. It is in this way that, again, 'lingua franca' merges with 'language', and it is not coincidental that the paradigm shift within ELF research is going precisely in this direction:

> It is hoped that with a larger ELF corpus [...] it will be possible not only to undertake more descriptive research but also pursue interesting perspectives for theorizing about the meaning of 'English(es)' and 'language' generally.
>
> (Seidlhofer, 2009, p. 242)

I agree that a better understanding of English as a lingua franca can offer ways to reconsider what we mean by 'English' and, more in general, 'language'. But I also think that the focus on formal linguistic features may be an obstacle that could impede the achievement of this goal. It is my persuasion that of ELF we do not need to know the *what*, but the *how* and the *why*. We need to understand how people position themselves towards it, how they locate it within their linguistic repertoire, how it contributes to shaping their identities and how they use it to participate in, or resist, aspects of globalisation. If world Englishes constitute an attitude, so should ELF, and, in a final analysis, the two can be seen as two terms denoting our laborious attempts to understand the unprecedented phenomenon of English in the world.

6
The Location of English in Malaysia

English = England!
Get the point?

—undergraduate Malaysian student

6.1 Introduction

Pramita is a young lecturer of English at a Malaysian university. Her family is of Panjabi origins and she grew up speaking Panjabi and English at home. She is also a very proficient user of Malay, which she learned when she went to school, and understands Hindi very well. Finally, exposure to Mandarin Chinese and Tamil has given her a rudimentary ability to understand these languages too. For a non-Malay Malaysian, Pramita's rich linguistic repertoire is not atypical. She states that, without doubt, English is the language she feels most comfortable with, as her command of Panjabi is limited by her inability to read or write in it and, generally, lack of regular practice. However, she is very resistant to calling English her mother tongue or admitting that she may be a native speaker of English. In Malaysia, the concept of 'mother tongue' is closely linked to ethnicity and ancestry, and therefore someone's mother tongue is automatically the language associated with the ethnic group he or she is considered to belong to. Hence, even if it is the language that one is brought up with at home, English is very unlikely to be regarded as that person's mother tongue and, concurrently, people will be very reluctant to consider themselves native speakers of English. A further complication in Pramita's case is that since most Malaysian Indians are of Tamil ethnico-linguistic origins, the language associated with the Indian section of Malaysian society is Tamil, of which Pramita has only a basic understanding. Thus, if taken as a whole, her multilingualism is the norm in her country (and in many other parts of the world) and can be understood as a natural result of the multilingual environment she lives and operates in. However, what the individual languages composing her linguistic repertoire *represent* to her is less clear. In particular, the location of English is ambiguous.

The problem is generated by the presence of intersecting identities. Pramita is a Malaysian Indian and, according to the general set-up of Malaysian society, this fact alone gives her two simultaneous identities: that of a Malaysian citizen and that of an ethnic Indian. The immediate linguistic implication is that she should, in theory, be a speaker of Malay, the country's national language, of Tamil, the language of the majority of Malaysian Indians, and of Panjabi, the language of her immediate ancestors. In actual fact, she uses English most of the time but, since in the wider Malaysian context the position of English is insecure, her own attitude towards the language is somewhat ambivalent.

It is significant, for example, that all the works of literature that she lists as her favourite are in English and that most of them are by American authors. Two of them are translations from other languages and only one is by a Malaysian author: a book that pokes fun at (stereo-)typically Malaysian behaviour. This seems to indicate two things: the first is a confirmation that English is indeed the language she uses most frequently and feels emotionally closest to; the second is that she appears to believe that good literature in English can only be found in America, but not in Asia. Considering the vastness of Asian (including Malaysian) literature in English and the growing recognition that it receives internationally, the latter point may be a little puzzling. Indeed, there is an odd contrast between Pramita's closeness to English in her daily life and the remoteness that she attributes to it as a literary language. This may well be a projection of the way she views herself as a user of English. Even though English is by far the main language she operates in, she does not consider it her native language and she does not see herself linguistically on a par with 'native speakers'. This encapsulates the idea that English is here but belongs elsewhere. It is as if she felt that she is borrowing a language from its true proprietors.

This anecdotal piece of information is emblematic of the location of English in Malaysia, a country with a variegated cultural, ethnic and linguistic ecology, where different ethnic groups, religions, languages, culinary traditions and music styles are distinctly visible and often intermix. Indeed, Malaysia's sociolinguistic landscape (see Omar, 1992) is rendered even more complex by the uneven and somewhat controversial presence of English and, in many ways, its sociolinguistic reality offers a miniature picture of a much wider situation worldwide, on the basis of the following characteristics:

- plurality of ethnic groups;
- plurality of religions;
- plurality of languages;
- diffused bi- and multilingualism, code-switching and code-mixing;
- presence of a national language, often used as a lingua franca, even if not uniformly, by the different groups;
- presence of English, cutting across all groups, but very unevenly distributed, sometimes preferred to the national language as a lingua franca, especially in the higher layers of society;
- ideological controversy over the English language in relation to its possible harmful effects to the national language.

These characteristics form an ideal environment where the discussion of the relocation of English can be both particularised and, at the same time, made relevant to a much broader and general context. In order to do this, I shall first describe the sociolinguistic landscape of Malaysia, and then discuss the uncertainties about the location of English in that landscape. The discussion is based on textual data about the ongoing debate over the role of English in the country as expressed in the national English-language press as well as the data that I collected through a survey conducted with 281 Malaysian students, in Malaysia in 2007 and in the United Kingdom in 2009. Table 6.1 and Table 6.2 below show details of my informants.

Table 6.1   Survey population according to age group and sex

		<18	18–27	>27	TOTAL
Malaysia, 2007	*Female*	11	122	34	167
	Male	7	58	4	69
	SUBTOTAL	18	180	38	236
UK, 2009	*Female*	0	30	0	30
	Male	0	15	0	15
	TOTAL	18	225	38	**281**

Table 6.2   Survey population according to ethnic group and level of education

		Malay	Chinese	Indian	TOTAL
Malaysia, 2007	*School*	35	33	14	82
	Undergraduate (UG)	64	58	9	131
	Postgraduate	5	0	18	23
	SUBTOTAL	104	91	41	236
UK, 2009	BEd TESL (UG)	36	5	4	45
	TOTAL	140	96	45	281

6.2   Malaysia's sociolinguistic landscape

The history of the Malay Peninsula has been marked by the arrival and settlement of a long succession of invaders and rulers of different origins: Indian, Chinese, Siamese and European. From a demographic point of view, this has caused a rich ethnic variety, while the original inhabitants of the territory are now only a small minority. The main feature that any Malaysian today is likely to mention about their country's population is that it is made up of three "races": Malay, Chinese and Indian. The word "race" sounds somewhat inappropriate to Western ears in this context and seems to be a relic of colonial discourse. In a periodical called *Journal of Negro Education*, William McLean wrote the following:

> Because of the great influx of Chinese and Indian immigrants, [Malaya] was peopled by three *races*; its social background was a conflicting medley because of its mixture of peoples.
>
> (McLean, 1946, p. 510)

The word 'immigrants' is rather misleading here, as many Chinese and Indians were actually brought to Malaya in the nineteenth and early twentieth centuries by the British to work in the country's two most important natural resources: tin and rubber. Indeed, the current composition of the Malaysian population is largely a result of those diasporas from southern China and southern India (even though Chinese and Indian presence in the Peninsula predates that period) through which the population, previously predominantly Malay and Muslim, became more variegated. Now, constituting just over 50 per cent of the population, the Malays are the largest ethnic group, followed by the Chinese, who account for about a quarter, and the Indians, who are slightly less than 10 per cent of the country's inhabitants. Indigenous groups, especially in East Malaysia, as well as recent immigrants from neighbouring countries, make up the rest of the country's population. The three larger groups are more heterogeneous than this simple classification suggests, but there are nevertheless some general traits that are applicable to a description of them. One is religion. The Malays are not only identified by ethnicity but also by religion, as they are fairly uniformly Muslim. Indeed, being a Muslim is considered to be an integral part of being a Malay. Although the link between ethnicity and religion is certainly looser for the other two groups, Chinese Malaysians are generally Taoists and/or Buddhists, while the Indians tend to be Hindus, with both minority groups including a small number of Christians. In addition, the Malays call themselves *bumiputra*, that is, 'children of the soil', to indicate that they were Malaysia's original inhabitants, predating the arrival of the Chinese and the Indians, and this special status grants them some privileges within Malaysian society.

Another trait which distinguishes the three ethnic groups to some extent is language. This is the area where things become particularly interesting for the central theme of this book. While, theoretically, all Malaysian citizens are expected to be proficient users of Malay, the national language is the mother tongue only for the Malays. Similar to what is the case with religion, the association of language and ethnic group is looser among the non-Malay portion of the population. The Chinese tend to speak Hokkien, Cantonese, Mandarin or other Chinese languages, while the Indians' mother tongue has traditionally been Tamil (since the ancestors of most Malaysian Indians originally came from the south-east of India), although other Indian languages are also present, such as Panjabi, Telegu, Hindi and others. Within this rich linguistic ecology bi- or multilingualism is very common, especially among non-Malays. In addition, what contributes significantly to making the collective linguistic repertoire much less neatly subdivided is the presence of English (Omar, 1994), which cuts across all ethnic groups, although it tends to be more frequently used by the affluent and more powerful groups.

6.3   English in the Malaysian sociolinguistic landscape

The territory that is now called Malaysia is a former British colony. The British began to take control of it in 1786 and, through various vicissitudes, came to administer it in its entirety in 1914. After the Second World War and the Japanese occupation, all the 11 states comprising the territory were united under the Malayan Union in 1946 and, shortly after, the Federation of Malaya in 1948. The Federation gained independence from Britain in 1957, while the current borders and name of Malaysia were established in 1963.

English in Malaysia has played an important role since colonial times, when it was the language of government, administration and commerce, and hence clearly the language of power. As they did in their other colonies, the British were keen that there would be an English-speaking elite and to this end they set up English-medium primary and secondary schools, which were often associated with prestige and were thought of as providing a "type and depth of knowledge [...] superior to that of the vernacular schools" (Gaudart, 1987). The English-medium schools were attended by children who later formed the ruling class of Malaysian society. In the meantime, the vast majority of the population did not have access to English and had substantially fewer opportunities for upward social mobility.

Because of its colonial past, according to Kachru's model of concentric circles, Malaysia belongs to the Outer Circle and English is supposedly a second language. This seems to be confirmed by my survey data. When asked to state whether they considered English a native language, a second language or a foreign language, nearly 90 per cent of my respondents said that it was a second language to them, 7.8 per cent a foreign language and 2.5 per cent a native language (Table 6.3).

However, as was discussed in Chapter 3, the three-circle classification is excessively simplistic and hence insufficient to describe and understand the roles and distribution of English in the world. The designation 'second language' may be too vague. Indeed, the depth and range of English in Malaysia are extremely uneven and, because of the country's heterogeneous sociolinguistic make-up, it is difficult to quantify with any precision the use of the English language. Abraham (2006, p. 16) reports that according to "the generally accepted 'estimate' [...] less than 5 per cent of the Malaysian population speak and actually use English in their day-to-day activities and in their normal daily life". This

Table 6.3   The roles of English according to Malaysian students

	Malay (%)	Chinese (%)	Indian (%)	TOTAL (%)
Native language	2.9	1.0	4.4	**2.5**
Second language	89.3	88.5	93.3	**89.7**
Foreign language	7.9	10.4	2.2	**7.8**

estimate seems to be rather conservative and its accuracy depends on what one means by "day-to-day activities" and "normal daily life". The percentage cited by Abraham is probably to be understood as referring to Malaysians who use English as their first language and only resort to using other languages when communicating with people who either do not speak or are not comfortable with English. These (first-language) L1 users of English tend to be highly educated, affluent urban professionals and, in general, people who belong to the social elite, regardless of ethnic background. They often will have received their education fully or partly in an Inner-Circle country and will typically send their children to private international schools. Below that upper layer of the Malaysian society, many people have a more or less sophisticated knowledge of English, especially in urban areas, where Chinese and Indian Malaysians occasionally prefer it to Malay as a lingua franca. In my own data, 9 per cent of the respondents said that they used English as their main language at home, 19 per cent with their friends and 30 per cent at school/university (Table 6.4).

McArthur (2002) estimates that about 20 per cent of the Malaysian population has functional knowledge of English. These figures, however, hide the discrepancies between urban areas and rural areas. In some contexts, the presence of English can be virtually nil. Within government organisations, Malay is routinely used and there is no pressing need for employees to be able to speak English. Similarly, in rural areas people do not find it necessary to speak English, as they prefer to use their mother tongue or a colloquial version of Malay as the lingua franca.

What is easier to quantify is the presence of English in the media. While the main language on Malaysian television is Malay, each station broadcasts English programmes with Malay subtitles for a few hours every day. Most English-language programmes are American, but some are also produced locally. At least six radio stations transmit programmes (mostly musical and talk shows) either partly, or completely, in English. The provision of English programmes is even broader on satellite TV. There are four national newspapers in English: *New Straits Times*, *The*

Table 6.4 The use of English as an L1 by Malaysian students

	Malay (%)	Chinese (%)	Indian (%)	TOTAL (%)
At home	8.7	2.2	24.4	**8.9**
At school/university	25.0	23.1	58.5	**30.1**
With friends	18.3	9.9	41.5	**19.1**

Star, The Malay Mail and *The Sun*. According to the Malaysian Audit Bureau of Circulations, in the period 2007–2008 there was an average of nearly 900,000 copies of English-language dailies in circulation, equivalent to 30 per cent of the total number (i.e. including the newspapers in other languages).

Generally, this lack of uniformity in the range and depth of use of English is fairly typical of postcolonial societies and it is probably also a reflection of the fact that after the Federation of Malaya gained independence from British colonial rule in 1957, English gradually lost its position both as the language of administration and as the language of education and entered a long phase marked by controversy and uncertainty.

6.4 Uncertainties and anxieties about English

From many points of view, the situation of post-independence Malaysia was not unlike that of many other countries that gained their independence from Britain in the 1950s and 1960s. Because of the ethnic, cultural, linguistic and religious plurality, it was a matter of urgency for the newly independent country that a strong sense of national identity would be felt by its citizens. As is always the case, one key element of national identity is the presence and use of a common national language. However, the linguistic and educational legacy left by the former colonisers was too fresh and strong to be done without and it was only in 1967, 10 years after independence, that the National Language Act proclaimed Malay, an indigenous language and an important lingua franca in the region, the sole official language of the country. During those years, the position of English as the inter-ethnic language of education for the elite had not changed much (Mandal, 2000, p. 1004).

The necessity to foster a sense of national unity in the population became much stronger after the racial riots that broke out in 1969. In 1970 the Malaysian Government implemented the National Education Policy, which enhanced the position of Malay as the national language and eventually phased out English as a medium of instruction in all public schools, with the exception of the Chinese and Tamil national-type primary schools (Pandian, 2002, p. 37). The Malay language took over in all aspects of administration and education and relegated English to a second language, taught like any other subject. According to Abraham (2006, p. 16), the switch to Malay ensured that there would be a rebalance in the opportunities that Malaysian people, and the Malays in particular, had to be educated, after a period when social inequalities "had the effect of demotivating them in [...] the acquisition of knowledge".

By 1983, the process reached the institutions of higher education, and by this time in theory, it was possible for Malaysian students to complete their studies entirely through Malay as the medium of instruction. In reality, the lack of resource materials in Malay made it necessary to retain English as a crucial reference language. Generally, however, even if English did not disappear completely, the reduction in its role and the corresponding enhancement of the role of Malay led to a decrease in the amount of students' exposure to English.

However, the downward trend of the English language in the country's official language policies was only one of the forces determining its fate in Malaysia. While the role of English was shifting from official language to second and even foreign language, the rapid economic growth that Malaysia had since the late 1970s, in conjunction with the increasingly globalised world economy and communication, ensured that there was a growing recognition of the importance of English for international trade, science and technology. Significantly, the Third Malaysia Plan (1975–1980) recognised that there was a need for Malaysians to be able to converse in English to help realise the country's aspiration of becoming an industrialised nation and the centre for regional education by 2020 (Schneider, 2003).

The awareness of the importance of possessing a working knowledge of English for Malaysians was coupled by a perception that the post-independence language policies had caused a general decline in Malaysians' level of proficiency in English. Educators expressed their concern that those who were educated exclusively through Malay would not able to master English sufficiently well and that, as a consequence, the Malays in particular were becoming monolingual. This was seen as an impediment for people's opportunities to find jobs in the private sector, where English was still widely used. More in general, there was fear that the country might lose its competitive edge in the era of globalised economy if people were not able to use English effectively to access knowledge and skills in science and technology. It was for this reason that in the 1990s English was re-instated for the teaching of scientific and technological subjects in higher education.

By the turn of the millennium the awareness became even more acute of the need to master English in order for the people of Malaysia to progress in all fields of life, especially in business, science and technology. The then Prime Minister Dr Mahathir Mohamad clearly stated,

To compete on equal terms with the world's most advanced countries, Malaysians – as well as most other Asian nationalities – still have some way to go. There are skills that must be learned and values that may yet have to change [...]. We have to learn the language of telecommunications, of computers, of the Internet.

(Mahathir, 1999, p. 40, cited in Foo and Richards, 2004, p. 237)

The position of English within the national curriculum was enhanced, including its role as a medium of instruction, until in May 2002 the Government announced a drastic change: English would replace Malay as the language of instruction for the teaching of science and mathematics in all primary and secondary schools across the country. This represented the highest point of the status of English in the gradual reverse of language policy in post-independence Malaysia. As such, the policy represented a victory for those who believed in the advantage of promoting English in the country. The support for it, however, was far from unanimous and the decision, which was put into practice in 2003, stirred a great deal of controversy and debate (Heng and H. Tan, 2006). In particular, those who were against it identified two types of problems: one of practical nature, the other more ideological. The practical issue was related to the abruptness of the change, as it required, in a relatively short time, the linguistic training of thousands of teachers who had never taught mathematics and science in English before, especially in rural areas. Hence, there were legitimate doubts of the feasibility and the effectiveness of the project. Without denying the challenge, those who were in favour of the change maintained that the difficulty would be only initial and that in the long run things would eventually fall into place.

The ideological issue was more complex and difficult to resolve. The discussion never really ceased and reached a climactic point in June/July 2009, when Malaysia was, once again, in the midst of a heated debate about the role of English in its education system and, by reflection, in its society. Six years after the policy was implemented, the Government decided to put a premature end to it. At the same time, the education authorities considered making English a compulsory 'pass' subject for the Sijil Pelajaran Malaysia (SPM), the national pre-university examination, partly in order to ensure that the presence of English in the national curriculum remained strong, but without eroding space from Malay. These changes in language policy might leave the external observer rather perplexed, who will not fail to notice how "the fortunes of English in Malaysia have waxed and waned and waxed again, and it never seems far from the centre of debate" (Pennycook, 1994, p. 217). A reader of the *New Straits Times* observed that the Malaysian Government did not seem to be clear on what status to assign to English, whether that of a second language or that of a foreign language:

> Teaching Maths and Science in English seemed to imply that Malaysia intended the status of English to be that of a second language for all students, while the recent announcement appears to relegate English to a foreign language, taught in schools, but likely to be truly mastered by only a few. This distinction now needs to be clarified [...]. Teachers, parents and students will need to be made aware of which of these is to be the model for Malaysia, and what the expectations are.
>
> ("Clarify English status", 2009)

The impression is that Malaysia is caught in an endless loop of hesitance and anxiety about how to best deal with the English language. That is, the location of English in Malaysia is still profoundly uncertain. The uncertainty is, for the most part, of ideological nature.

6.5   The ideological conundrum

For the last 50 years, the status to be accorded to the English language in Malaysia has been the subject of debate, and the position that English should occupy within the linguistic ecology of the country has never been conclusively established. In particular, the fulcrum of the discussion has been at the intersection of two forces: (a) the will to preserve and support Malay as the national language and the symbol of national unity; (b) the recognition of English as an indispensable language in a globalised economy. Generally speaking, the prevalence of one or the other force has resulted in changes in language policies, either pro-Malay or pro-English. Those who belong to the pro-Malay (and anti-English) camp express the preoccupation that if English played an excessively important role in people's lives, it would erode space from the national language, and that the relegation of Malay to a secondary position would then have a consequent detrimental effect for the unity of the nation and the preservation of Malay culture. Moreover, as it tends to be a prerogative of the urban, wealthier segment of the population, the use of English is seen as an element of further discrimination towards the poorer rural people, who would find themselves even more disadvantaged. Finally, the association of English with the former colonial masters and with Christianity still generates resistance in certain sections of the Malaysian society. The Sekretariat Himpunan Ulama' Rantau Asia (SHURA), an association of Islamic scholars, for example, called for the abolition of the use of English for the teaching of mathematics and science, defining it "harmful for the nation's youth" ("PPSMI wajib dimansuh", 2009). More generally, the pro-Malay are keen for Malaysian citizens to bear in mind that the country should have "one official language in whatever that you do, which is Bahasa Malaysia, as enshrined in the Constitution" ("No doubting BM's relevance", 2009).

The pro-English front is formed by those who, pragmatically, feel that knowledge of English is an invaluable asset for Malaysians, especially if the country aspires to participate successfully in the global economy. They seek to persuade the sceptics that the English language cannot do any harm to the Malay language and/or culture and that it ought to be viewed in an ideology-free manner. One of the most common forms of reassurance put forward by those who wish to boost the use of English in Malaysia is that speaking English does not mean *being* English or embracing Western cultural values. Former Malaysian Prime Minister Dr Mahathir Mohamad, historically one of the staunchest supporters of the promotion of English in his country, posited the following: "We do not become European simply because we wear a coat and a tie, speak English and practise democracy instead of feudalism" (Mahathir, 1999, p. 40, cited in Foo and Richards, 2004, p. 237). This is an opinion that is frequently voiced by pro-English Malaysians in the national press. The following extract from a letter sent by a reader to the English-language newspaper the *New Straits Times* makes the point explicitly:

We must not regard the learning and mastery of the English language as a threat to our culture or national identity. [...]. Mastering English does not make one less Malay, Chinese, Indian or Malaysian. Mastering English is about rejuvenating the nation. It is about preparing ourselves individually and collectively as a nation in finding our place in the global economy. Promoting English would not in any way jeopardise the importance and use of Bahasa Malaysia as our national and official language. Improving the standard of English will not diminish the importance of our national language, since bilingualism or even trilingualism is an unwritten need for social and professional competence in this age.

("Give them a choice of schools", 2009)

The same message was expressed particularly emphatically by Her Royal Highness Raja Zarith Sofia Idris, Crown Princess of Johor, in a lecture she gave at the opening ceremony of the 18th MELTA International Conference (11 June 2009). The Princess reiterated the importance for Malaysians to master the English language if the country was to be competitive in today's globalised world and, in order to dissipate fears that English might harm Malaysians' sense of national identity and culture, she explained that using the English language did not have to equate to becoming anglicised or unpatriotic:

> It has nothing to do with being pro-English or pro-British. It has nothing to do with glorifying our British colonial past. It has nothing to do with us being any less nationalistic or patriotic. [...] We do not have to fear the English language: studying English as a language won't change us from being Malaysians to being pseudo-English, or pseudo-Americans, or pseudo-other native English speakers.
>
> (HRH Raja Zarith Sofia Idris, 2009)

The point that the promoters of English in Malaysia are adamant to make is that one can speak English without altering one's own national, cultural or religious identity. Yet, the perseverance of the debate and the recent reversal of policy on English as a medium of instruction (see Section 6.4) demonstrate that the argument does not succeed in persuading those who view the English language as an alien intruder and a cause of social inequality. It is possible that the argument is not made strongly enough. However, I am of the opinion that the pro-English discourse is too fundamentally contradictory. On the one hand, it overtly claims that speaking English does not need to involve any contingent affinity with Western people, their beliefs, values, behaviours or ways of life. On the other hand, however, more implicitly it continues to reinforce a subliminal link between English and a location which is both physically and spiritually far and detached from the Malaysian cultural context. If the detractors of English see it as extraneous to the Malaysian nation, the promoters do not really see it otherwise. In fact, both schools of thought equally deny the relocation of English away from the Inner Circle and into Malaysia.

6.6   Reaffirming the English–England connection

HRH Raja Zarith Sofia Idris' lecture is a fitting example. In order to illustrate the concept that speaking English is not equivalent to embracing English and/or Western culture, the Princess referred to her own experience and, in particular, to the 10 years when she received her secondary and higher education in England. During those years, she reported, her Malaysian identity was not affected by the Western environment that surrounded her. As evidence of the firmness of her cultural stronghold, she cited the fact that, while in England, she was never tempted to dye her hair blond or wear blue-tinted contact lenses. She also assured her audience that, even more importantly, she continued to crave for and eat Malaysian food and, as a further confirmation of her unscathed anti-imperialist convictions, she remarked how European mouldy cheese smelled just as bad to Asians as did Malaysian *sambal belacan* (prawn paste) to Westerners.

The lecture was delivered in an informal way and was enlivened by amusing anecdotes, but the question must be addressed at a much deeper level. The first and most obvious objection that can be made is that if wearing a tie does not turn an Asian into a European, refraining from eating cheese does not necessarily safeguard one from being Europeanised. However, the real crux of the matter is that the strong psychological association between English the language and England the country is not challenged. By using her experience as an illustrative example of the point she wished to make, the Princess implicitly made a series of important and deeply significant statements. In her lecture she talked about two interconnected themes: (a) the importance of mastering the English language because of the benefits it can offer to people, (b) her own experience as a student in England as evidence of the fact that speaking English does not turn one into an English person. One result of this thematic structure is the strengthening of the connection between the physical location England and the language English, thereby reinforcing the idea that the closeness between the two names is more than just a matter of morphology: *Engl*ish is unequivocally the language of *Engl*and. Moreover, another existing belief that is corroborated is that England is not only the home of the English language, but also the place where the best education is available. Very significantly, the degree that the Princess studied for at the University of Oxford was in Chinese Studies (while she admitted having never been to China), manifestly indicating that England is the best place to acquire knowledge, even about something intrinsically Asian. Indeed, in the closing ceremony of the conference, the Princess added that Malaysians' "mastery of the language will help them become confident writers and speakers" and "this will enable them to exchange ideas, take part in discussions and debates and study at good universities in native

English-speaking countries." If these countries, with Britain at the top, are the places where universal knowledge resides and is best imparted, access to good education is granted by the combination of (a) the ability to speak English and (b) the financial means necessary to afford studying at expensive universities in the Inner Circle.

Consequently, the argument about the pragmatic usefulness and desirability of mastering English is embedded within a broader discourse which effectively reinforces a matrix of existing associations between the English language and other variables in the equation, as illustrated in Figure 6.1. It is for this reason that the pro-English argument is, to say the least, unlikely to placate the preoccupations of those who fear that the use of English in education creates imbalance in the Malaysian society.

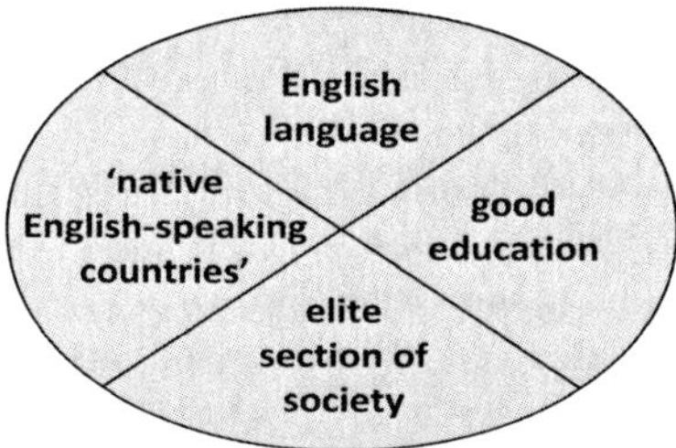

Figure 6.1   The English language matrix

The Princess' lecture is emblematic of a sentiment which is shared by many English-using Malaysians, whose discourse exhibits, and contributes to producing, the matrix of associations represented above. In the pro-English discourse, speaking English is more than just speaking a language. A reader of the English-language newspaper *The Star* lamented Malaysians' insufficient impact in the world scene:

> Our citizens are well-educated and skilful but yet we find that our impact to the world does not appear to commensurate with this level of literacy. [...] I suggest that the reason is we don't speak, think and act in the language of the world, which is English.
>
> ("Well-educated but not literate in English", 2009)

Speaking English is not enough: it is necessary to think and act in English too. Fanon's statement remains intact.

The idea that learning English is important in order to be able to attend good foreign universities in the Inner Circle is also a common one. With reference to a suggestion made by the Education Minister that

English be made a compulsory 'pass' subject in the SPM examination, another reader of *The Star* commented the following:

> [...] the level of English in universities in Britain is high. [...] I completed the IB programme in a British international school in Thailand which has provided me a good foundation in the English language. [...] By making English a 'must pass' subject, it will definitely help those who wish to further their studies in the universities since courses are taught in English.
>
> ("English can help breach 'international barrier' ", 2009)

For this reader, who was studying for a Master's Degree in London when he posted his letter, the ability to study in foreign universities was the primary reason for having a good command of English. It is significant that he chose to receive his pre-university education in a 'British international school' in Thailand, a country where the presence of English is rather sparse in comparison to Malaysia. Evidently, he must have considered the 'British' designation of the school a guarantee of good quality. Similarly, another reader of *The Star* contended that it would be a good idea to

> open up more schools with English as the medium of instruction, [since] by doing so, we would automatically have a larger "English-speaking population" who would have no problems sitting for stringent entry tests when they apply to foreign universities.
>
> ("Open up more English schools", 2009)

English is frequently seen as synonymous to access to knowledge and good education. According to another reader of *The Star*, in order to argue for the necessity to keep high the level of education through English, she noted how many present and past world leaders were 'English-educated':

> Our Tunku Abdul Rahman and all our other Prime Ministers and world leaders like Mahatma Gandhi, Jawaharlal Nehru and Nelson Mandela were patriotic despite their having been wholly or largely English-educated.
>
> ("Why the need to go English", 2009)

Here, "English-educated" does not just mean educated through English as a medium of instruction, it also means educated in England or in the English education system. Incidentally, the mention of world leaders makes the association of English with the elite even more overt. Being able to study at an Inner-Circle university is one of the reasons for studying English for many Malaysians. In my survey the ability to study in an Inner-Circe country received an average score of 3.06, which was the fifth highest-rated reason indicated by the participants (see Table 6.5).

On the one hand, the data indicate a very pragmatic and instrumental orientation towards English, as the vast majority of my respondents believed that the ability to use English is of crucial importance in the job market. On the other hand, they also suggest a view of English as a language projected towards the external world, strongly connected to the Inner Circle but with negligible local function. There is hardly any indication that English may be considered a Malaysian language. Interestingly, this appears to be in line with a study of the Malaysian press conducted by Peter Tan (2005), whose aim was to try and establish which phase of development had been reached by Malaysian English. In doing so, Tan referred to Schneider's 'dynamic model' (Schneider, 2003, 2007), according to which varieties of English in postcolonial contexts may go through five phases of development: (1) foundation, (2) exonormative stabilisation, (3) nativisation, (4) endonormative stabilisation and (5) differentiation. He found that there was scarce evidence that English might have been appropriated by Malaysians as a national language. Given the complexity of the country's sociolinguistic reality, it was extremely difficult for Tan's study to come to any firm conclusion about the stage of development of Malaysian English. Tan, however, does suggest that the indecisions are not too wide-ranging, as they "involve assigning Malaysia into phase 3 or phase 4 of the framework" (2005, p. 61). I would be more cautious, as both my data and my impressionistic personal experience tend to rule out the possibility that English in Malaysia may be going through a phase of endonormative

Table 6.5   Malaysian students' top five reasons for studying English

	Malay	Chinese	Indian	TOTAL
Career prospects	3.90	3.78	3.93	**3.86**
Communication with people from other countries	3.54	3.52	3.54	**3.53**
Communication with native speakers	3.39	3.32	3.20	**3.33**
Knowledge in science and technology	3.35	2.77	3.20	**3.10**
Studying in an Inner-Circle country	3.31	2.91	2.76	**3.06**

stabilisation. This is largely because of the general low esteem that many English-using Malaysians have of the way English is used in their country.

6.7   *Bahasa rojak* and the myth of pure English

The low esteem of one's own variety of the language left by former colonisers is, after all, not atypical in postcolonial situations. In describing the situation in Hong Kong, Joseph (2004, pp. 132–161) observes how there is hardly any recognition of a valid local variety of English among Hong Kong English speakers:

> The first thing they would deny is that they speak something that ought to be identified as 'Hong Kong English'. With few exceptions, it is linguists who talk about this language. Its speakers scoff at the notion that there is anything other than 'good English' (represented by the overseas standard) and the 'bad English' of their compatriots.
>
> (2004, p. 139)

In Malaysia the recognition of at least the existence of something called 'Malaysian English' is much more discernible, even though the opinion about its quality and validity is equally very low. Table 6.6 below shows the percentage of my informants who recognised the existence of Malaysian English compared to the percentage of those who felt that it was as good as Inner-Circle varieties of English.

While well over 90 per cent of my respondents did acknowledge Malaysian English as a linguistic entity, just above a quarter of them thought that it was on the same level of quality as Inner-Circle varieties. The breakdown of the data according to age groups shows a very clear trend, whereby younger Malaysians seem to be much less confident than their older counterparts about the quality of Malaysian English. If Malaysian English did not encounter much favour, the variety of English that was deemed the most suitable to be used as a model in education

Table 6.6   Malaysian students' recognition and evaluation of Malaysian English

	<18 (%)	18–27 (%)	>27 (%)	TOTAL (%)
Malaysian English exists	94.4	91.6	100.0	**92.9**
Malaysian English is as good as Inner-Circle varieties	0.0	25.30	55.3	**27.8**

Table 6.7   Varieties of English suitable to be taught in Malaysia

	<18 (%)	18–27 (%)	>27 (%)	TOTAL (%)
British English	22.2	68.4	71.1	**65.8**
American English	77.8	22.2	7.9	**23.8**
Malaysian English	0.0	10.2	7.9	**9.3**
Others	0.0	2.2	2.6	**2.1**

was British English, with a significantly higher percentage of preference received in comparison to American English (Table 6.7).

As the table shows, less than 10 per cent of my respondents felt that Malaysian English could be used as a model for teaching, confirming the very low regard of it. Two-thirds thought that British English was the most suitable variety to be taught in Malaysia, although there seems to be a clear tendency for younger Malaysians to favour American English. In general, those who indicated British English as their choice gave the following reasons (see also Table 6.8):

- *Quality*: British English is the correct/standard version of English
- *History*: Malaysia is a former British colony and British English has traditionally been taught here; also, Britain is where English originally developed
- *Diffusion*: British English is the most widely recognised variety of English
- *Intelligibility*: British English is the easiest variety to understand

The predilection for British English is the specular image of the disapproval of Malaysian English, to the extent that there is a positive–negative polar opposition in the perception of the two varieties of English. When attached to the noun 'English', the adjective 'Malaysian' becomes almost a synonym of 'poor' or 'sub-standard'. Indeed, many English-using Malaysians comment negatively on the quality of English

Table 6.8   Reasons for favouring British English

Quality	**29.4%**
History	**15.7%**
Intelligibility	**17.0%**
Diffusion	**12.4%**
Other reasons	**6.5%**
None given	**19.0%**

used in their country. In the 1980s, Gaudart already observed that the "Malaysian society is constantly regaled with opinions about the falling standards of English. Falling where and in what way is seldom mentioned" (1987, p. 1). More than two decades later, the situation has not changed, and comments on the falling standards of English are very common. Below is just a small sample of such comments appeared between June and August 2009 on the online versions of *The Star* and the *New Straits Times*:

The Star

- "The standard of English as a written and oral language has dropped in Malaysia" ("If you fail English, no SPM certificate", 2009).
- "The standard of English [has] dropped to pathetic levels over the past 30 year" ("On making a pass in English compulsory in SPM", 2009).
- "The general level of English proficiency [...] declined alarmingly" ("Why the need to go English", 2009).
- "The level of English has already gone down the drain" (Wong, 2009).
- "Over the last two decades the standard of English in the country has been on the decline" ("English for maths and science", 2009).

New Straits Times

- "Malaysia, with a first-class foundation in English at one time (that is, my time), is now going downhill (in respect of English) at an accelerated pace" ("Simply the language of the world", 2009).
- "[...] the deteriorating standard of English competency among our people" ("Bring the fun back to the teaching of English", 2009).
- "English-proficiency standards have hit rock bottom among our schoolchildren and university graduates" ("Audit first", 2009).
- "The standard of English in Malaysia has dropped shockingly" ("It's the teachers who are failing us", 2009).
- "The standard of English in this country has dropped miserably" ("Get students started on the basics", 2009).

With particular reference to the Hong Kong context, Joseph (2004, pp. 134–139; 2006, pp. 36–39) makes the point that the perception of 'falling standards' felt by a significant number of older English-using people in Hong Kong is one way of looking at exactly the same phenomenon of language change that linguists are keen to regard as the emergence of a new variety of English. In Malaysia this is also the case. However, what is of significance is that here the discourse of 'falling standards' makes explicit reference to the Malaysianisation of English as the primary index of deterioration. The fault, that is, tends to be attributed to what is often referred to as *bahasa rojak* (*bahasa* is 'language' and *rojak* 'mixture' in Malay), whereby 'good English' is English that has not been tainted by what is viewed as negative interference from local languages, and 'bad English' is English with a distinct local flavour.

Referring to the Malaysian press, Tan observed that "The kind of dynamics [...] where English co-exists with other languages and where English could be appropriated and Malaysianised is not envisaged" (Tan, 2005, p. 60). Indeed, not only is it not envisaged, but the Malaysianisation of English is often vociferously condemned and rejected. One of the most frequent objections to the way Malaysians use English relates to the phenomena of code-switching and code-mixing, two 'sins' whose allegedly deplorable nature is predicated but never really explained. A popular belief is that they cause linguistic degeneration. *The Star* columnist and TV writer Dzof Azmi admits with guilt to falling into the language-mix temptation:

> [M]uch of what I do is in English. I write in Malay when I write scripts for Malaysian television, but even then, discussion of these ideas degenerates into some rojak melange of the two languages.
>
> (Azmi, 2009)

A virtual synonym of *bahasa rojak* is the equally uncomplimentary 'Manglish', a word whose morphology is equivalent to that of 'Singlish', 'Chinglish', 'Hinglish', 'Spanglish' and so on and emphasises the *rojak* nature of the language. Whichever term is used, the mixing of English with local languages is routinely considered an inexcusable transgression. Another reader of *The Star*, for example, argued for the promotion of bilingualism in her country, by which she meant the ability of people to use Malay and English with the same level of proficiency and confidence. Like many other pro-English individuals, she contended that "the importance of the English language [...] in no way den[ies] the position of Bahasa Malaysia as the national language" and that "Malaysians must be fluent speakers who can express their thoughts articulately in both languages." However, she warned, it was imperative that the two languages be kept separated from one another: "[Malaysians] must be able to use each language confidently and consistently at all level of discourse, NOT in the mumbo-jumbo of Manglish, bahasa rojak or pidgin!" ("Bilingualism is the way to go", 2009).

Mixing Malay and English was identified as a major cause for linguistic deterioration in schools by another reader of *The Star*:

The communicative approach has not been effective to make children speak correct English. We observe that most children in school these days speak a mixture of English and Malay or other languages. Over 95% of our school going children speak Manglish and code-switching is very common. Even teachers do this, without realising it.
("Grammar drilling will help weak students", 2009)

The reader here makes a clear distinction between 'correct English' and 'Manglish'. It is interesting that the communicative approach, with its focus on meaning rather than on form, has been identified as the perpetrator of code-switching. The same reader wrote a letter to the *New Straits Times*, condemning the use of 'Manglish' in Malaysian media and on the Internet:

The dialogue used in [American computer games and cartoons] is in proper English, as opposed to the language used by some teachers in the classroom. They [*sic*] are authentic and not Manglish. I cannot say the same for some of our local television and radio programmes. Just listen to the deejays using Manglish, ending their discourse with the suffix "lah". [...]. [Malaysians' language skills] are getting worse with the advent of new communication technologies and the creation of e-mail and SMS language, the use of short forms, acronyms and abbreviations; the mixing of Malay and English colloquial language and slang [...]. One has to look at the chats and comments on Facebook and Twitter, e-mails and blogs to realise the extent of linguistic deterioration.
("Manglish spanner in the works", 2009)

Some commentators go to great lengths to explain the 'mistakes' that Malaysians commit when they speak English. This tends to happen, for example, in a section of *The Star* called 'Mind our English', where contributors offer advice and answer questions on various aspects of English language use. It is without doubt a very useful regular column, but sometimes emphasis on 'correctness' overshadows the importance of intelligibility and, above all, ignores the features that English has acquired locally and have become *de facto* standard. For example, one contributor explained that, according to her, Malaysians do not use question tags correctly. The feature she was referring to is the reduction of the number of question tags to just one or two: *is it?* and/or its negative equivalent *isn't it?* This is one of the most common characteristics of many Englishes around the world, including in Britain, and it is standard in Malaysia and Singapore, causing no problems of intelligibility. Indeed, like most forms of natural linguistic simplification, it *enhances* intelligibility: it is easier to understand and to say *isn't it?* than *mightn't we?* And yet, this writer of 'Mind our English' felt that this simplified use of question tags was ungrammatical and 'non-standard'. Intelligibility, however, was not a tenable justification: "The message in such questions is clear enough, but the grammar does not pass muster" ("What's the question again?", 2009), as if the Grammar were a kind of divine code that must be obeyed without question.

These readers belong to the group of people who welcome English as beneficial to Malaysian society and seek to persuade their compatriots that the presence of this language does not necessarily harm the Malay language and culture. Yet, within this optic, English is sanctified as a precious object, whose pure beauty is to be respected and never adulterated through contact with a local language. The moment it brushes against the rich and variegated Malaysian culture, English 'degenerates' into 'Manglish'. The ubiquitous particle *lah*, a common discourse marker in Malaysia, Singapore and Hong Kong, is often mentioned, almost as a symbol of the contamination of 'Manglish'. A concerned reader of *The Star* laments the excessive use of it:

> It seems that many Malaysians nowadays are using the word *lah* to end a sentence, even when they are speaking English. Please encourage the use of proper words and sentences in our daily conversation. Make a change today. I am confident others will do the same. Although we call it Malaysian English, we shouldn't encourage our future generations to continue such a habit as it doesn't encourage proper usage of the English language. I am also encouraging teachers and lecturers to stop using the word *lah*.
>
> ("Discourage use of 'lah' in English", 2009)

As is typical of such comments, no explanation is given as to why words, no matter how small, from local languages should not be used, apart from the claim that they make English 'incorrect', even though they do not hinder an outsider's understanding of it. Indeed, intelligibility is not normally an issue. 'Proper English' becomes equivalent to 'pure English', that is, English that is not contaminated by Malaysian ingredients. It is interesting how this idealised form of de-Malaysianised English is seen as authentic and relevant, whereas 'Manglish' is impure, incorrect and, therefore, inauthentic. With regard to the same topic, another reader of *The Star* expressed dissatisfaction with Malaysians' 'complacent mindset':

> Many of us fail to improve our English because of a complacent mind-set. We ignore grammar and include lots of Malay and Chinese words such as *lah, arr, hor* or *de* instead of using standard English expressions to convey our thoughts and feelings. We think this is fine as long as our Manglish is understood by others.
>
> ("What's there to boast when we're speaking Manglish?", 2009)

This is an extremely interesting remark because, unlike other comments, it does mention intelligibility, and it places it in a relation of oppositeness with correctness: the attainment of the former is inconsequential if the latter is not guaranteed. In fact, it is *wrong* to think that intelligibility is, really, what counts.

Criticism towards Malaysians' English is also occasionally expressed by 'native speakers' of the language. These tend to be Britons, Australians, Americans and so on who reside in Malaysia, often as English language teachers or 'experts'. Some of them, from time to time, feel the need to castigate Malaysians' use of English. Moved by such intent, one Englishman offered some of his linguistic wisdom in *The Star*, again about the use of particles such as *lah, arr, mah* and so on:

> Firstly, not all Malaysians use the terms. It is predominantly a practice among the Chinese. So, it doesn't actually make you a Malaysian at all. There is nothing to be proud of in using these meaningless expressions. Secondly, such sloppy terms do not exactly set a good example to our children who would prefer to know proper English. [...] We should not be proud of "Manglish". Rather, it is a blemish to the country and hinders its population from knowing proper English.
>
> ("Say, it will be nice if we aren't proud of Manglish", 2009)

That such particles are exclusively used by the Malaysian Chinese is factually incorrect. However, what is more interesting is that the reader considers them an index of sloppiness and, in line with other similar comments, an element of disturbance in what should otherwise be 'proper English'. Once more, there is no reference to intelligibility, which is not even contemplated as being of any relevance in a discussion about language use.

An Australian contributor to 'Mind our English' wrote an article listing a number of 'mistakes' allegedly made by Malaysians. The article ("Only in Malaysia", 2009) expresses perfectly well a mental attitude which denies the possibility that English, or any language, may be more ductile than a granitic monolith, and ignores the fact that dealing with unfamiliar linguistic features is generally a matter of accommodation and meaning negotiation. The so-called mistakes catalogued in the article are standard expressions in Malaysia and Singapore and the outsider does not require more than one or two encounters to realise what their meanings are, especially in the context in which they are used. The expressions in question are listed in Table 6.9, alongside alternatives illustrating their meanings for those who are not familiar with them.

The contributor also commented on the confusion that Malaysians apparently display between *to bring* and *to take* and between *to borrow* and, as she put it, *to loan*. They are both classic TESOL textbook cases. In reality, that is, outside the TESOL classroom, the difference between *to bring* and *to take* is often indistinct and semantically quite immaterial, while the use of *to borrow* in place of *to loan* or, more commonly, *to lend* may be frowned upon by those who assign to themselves the role of guardians of English, but is in fact a natural simplification resulting from the fact that many languages use the same verb for what is effectively the same meaning.

The author of the article, who had lived in Malaysia for 8 years at the time of writing, obviously knew what all those expressions meant and, indeed, her contribution to 'Mind our English' recounts the feeling of puzzlement she had the *first* time she heard them. The English language

Table 6.9 'Mistakes' made by Malaysians

English expression in Malaysia	Alternative expression
To follow someone somewhere	*To drive someone somewhere*
To send someone somewhere/back	*To drive somewhere/home*
To open/close the light	*To turn on/off the light*
Last time	*In the past*
To spend someone lunch	*To buy someone lunch*
To take (beef, pork, etc.)	*To eat (beef, pork, etc.;* especially used in questions, given the existence of various religious restrictions)
To see first	*To consider the matter first* (before taking a decision)

does not have, and has never had, a code of conduct, and the 'mistake' nature of linguistic expressions that we do not approve of but are used by everybody else around us is entirely a product of our own mental attitude. Significantly, after so many years in the country, she was still battled by a linguistic dilemma: "I'm not sure whether I should work myself to death to try and change these mistakes or simply start using them myself" ("Only in Malaysia", 2009). Clearly, by writing the article, she decided that it would be worth trying to change those 'mistakes' rather than changing her attitude and recognising the variability and adaptability of the English language.

Thus, the common belief, expressed by English-using Malaysians and 'expats' alike, can be summarised in the following two points:

- Malaysians' English is faulty due to the interferences from local languages;
- in order to rectify the situation it is necessary to keep English as free as possible of such interferences.

One consequence of this axiom is that those who are thought of as using English at its best are monolingual speakers from the Inner Circle, since they are far enough from the corrupting influence of the Malaysian cultural melting pot. Accordingly, the pro-English discourse makes frequent references to the desirability to emulate 'native speakers'. One of the readers of *The Star* mentioned above, for example, recommends that Malaysian students can improve and purify their English by using language tapes which would give them a chance to "get to hear English spoken by native speakers in conversations and in relevant communicative situations" ("Bilingualism is the way to go", 2009). Similarly, according to a reader of the *New Straits Times*, the only way to improve one's English is by exposure to 'native speakers', an opportunity not available in Malaysia:

> You have to listen to the way [English] is being spoken by native speakers. [...]. Malaysia is not an English-speaking country. [...]. How can we blame teachers for not being fluent in the English language when they do not have the opportunity to listen to good conversations by native speakers and read good sentence constructions.
> ("No doubting BM's relevance", 2009)

The conviction that 'native speakers' may help raise the standard of English in Malaysia is also shared by the Government. In expressing the intention to foster the teaching of English in the country, for example, Malaysia's deputy Prime Minister and Education Minister Tan Sri Muhyiddin Yassin stated,

> Beginning 2012, we will extend English hours in schools and get the best teachers to teach English, including those from English-speaking countries. Our students will then have the experience of communicating with native speakers of English. We hope this will further improve their command of the language.
>
> (Abas and Hamid, 2009)

This decision was endorsed by another reader of *The Star*, who urged policy-makers not to hesitate and "hire the necessary number of teachers from native English-speaking countries" ("English can help launch Malaysia to next level of growth", 2009).

6.8 Conclusion

It is clear that the myth of 'pure English' is very prominent in the pro-English discourse in the press. It is based on a binary opposition with 'Manglish':

'Manglish'	'Pure English'
Incorrect	Correct
Non-standard	Standard
Unintelligible	Intelligible
Vulgar	Refined
Spoken by Malaysians	Spoken by 'native speakers'
Malaysianised	Free of Malaysian interferences

The 'myth' both generates and is a reflection of a conceptualisation of English which locates and keeps the language firmly outside the borders of the Malaysian sociolinguistic reality. It denies any form of relocation of English out of the Inner Circle, and so English remains a language that belongs to, and is therefore borrowed from, the Native Speaker. As such, it must be treated with utmost care and not allowed to be dirtied by the contamination of local languages. This refusal to relocate English from its ancestral home, the idea of English as a gift and the anxiety to keep it untouched by anything local, I say not without hesitation, may contain residues of colonial mentality. HRH Raja Zarith Sofia Idris recommended that Malaysians "must dissociate [their] willingness to study the English language from any kind of hidden political or social agendas" (2009) but the problem is that the pro-English discourse is impregnated with nuances which are both political and social. Sometimes the rhetoric of the promoters of English acquires even explicit racial tones:

> We should go for English unless we have decided to go backwards instead of forward [...]. We do not need to be specialised or to speak like the white men, but at least a proficiency in the English language should be a must.
>
> ("Even China banking on English", 2009)

This is a sociopolitical statement. The use of the expression 'white men' typifies a series of deep-rooted beliefs. First of all, that 'white men' are expert users of English. Secondly, 'white men' is used as a synonym of 'native speakers', indicating that the notion 'native speaker' is based on ethnicity. Also, the expertise that 'white men'/'native speakers' are graced with is totally taken for granted, as if it were in their genes. Finally, there is the conviction that whoever is *not* a white/native speaker cannot really reach the white man's innate level of expertise. This is a statement that, more or less overtly, is made repeatedly. The following extracts are exemplary. A reader of *The Star* asked the following:

> I'm curious about how we can get rid of our Malaysian accent and speak with a British or American accent. I tried in many ways to change my accent but they didn't work at all. Why is it that Westerners like the French and the Spanish can speak English easily without any accent but not us Asians?
>
> ("How do I get rid of my accent?", 2009)

The desire to speak with a British or American accent is in line with the myth of 'pure English' discussed above, but what is more interesting here is the assumption that Westerners (i.e. white people) are believed to be able to speak English "easily without any accent", unlike Asians, who, apparently, cannot. The reference to ethnicity is therefore still very obvious. The answer to the reader's question contains a common form of more subtle preconception:

> I don't think we should try too hard to sound British or American when we speak. We should just try to pronounce the words as

correctly and clearly as we can, so that English speakers from other countries can understand us – and then speak naturally. Never mind if our intonation sounds somewhat Chinese, Malay or Indian. Malaysians who try too hard to sound British or American can end up sounding funny rather than impressive!

("How do I get rid of my accent?", 2009)

In other words, sounding British or American *would* be desirable but, unfortunately, it is an aim that Malaysians are not able to reach and therefore it is not worthwhile for them to try too hard. In fact, when they do try hard, they only end up sounding funny. For this reason, they should settle for a clear pronunciation that can be understood by others, even if, never mind, it sounds Chinese, Malay or Indian. This type of advice supposedly shows open-mindedness towards English but it actually contains the same kind of deference towards the 'native speakers' displayed in the reader's question.

I am conscious that I have painted a rather negative picture of the pro-English discourse in Malaysia. It is not meant as a generalisation, but as a way of teasing out certain profound contradictions which, in my opinion, cause the dilemmas and uncertainties about English to continue *ad infinitum*. With its emphasis on the necessity for Malaysians to 'purify' and de-Malaysianise English, the pro-English discourse has influenced the younger generations, who seem to have very little confidence in the validity of Malaysian English and regard British or American models as more suitable for their education.

Of course, there are also other voices and other viewpoints beyond and alternative to those I have taken into consideration thus far. Mandal, for example, observes the following:

With a relatively lengthy educational, institutional and literary tradition in the country, the English language has been an important site for negotiating the colonial past and configuring a political community without respect to ethnic and cultural difference.

(Mandal, 2000, p. 1003)

I have profound respect for statements of this type and I do not doubt their truthfulness. They are aligned with the tradition of World Englishes literature, which often refers, for example, to a country's literary production in order to find acts of resistance, nonconformity and so on performed through instances of appropriation of English. Indeed, in order to illustrate his point, Mandal cites three Malaysian creative writers, one of whom is Salleh Ben Joned, who is very clear about what English should represent for Malaysians:

> A language belongs to those who speak it. It's as simple as that. Given this fact, and that language communicates experience and is capable of transcending the boundaries of the culture of its origin – given all this, then the English we speak belongs to us. It's our English; along with [Malay] it expresses our 'soul', with all its contradictions and confusions, as much as our social and material needs.
>
> (Joned, 1994, p. 65)

The problem is that these processes of appropriation of English, real and fascinating as they may be, tend to be confined within relatively restricted literary and scholarly domains and cannot be said to represent the broader consciousness of an entire population. The negotiation of the colonial past through the English language may have configured a political community but such community is, nonetheless, an elite group. As Tupas acutely observes,

> [...] the power to (re)create English ascribed to the Outer Circle is mainly reserved only to those who have been invested with such power in the first place (the educated/the rich/the creative writers, etc.) such that the Inner/Outer dichotomy is demolished by the fact that no matter what standards of English are used, the power to deploy such standards is shared by both 'native' and 'non-native' speakers who enjoy particular social privileges such as wealth, symbolic power, education, and so on, in their respective communities or societies.
>
> (2006, pp. 169–170)

In addition, as Annamalai (2005) has noted, divergent forms of English actually represent a social disadvantage for members of lower classes and it is entirely "a matter of political ideology whether such 'deficient' English is interpreted as a subversive act" (p. 34). Similarly, Ramanathan (2005) has underlined how "English [...] is entrenched in the heart of a class-based divide" (p. vii).

However, it is possible that the reconfiguration of the English language that goes on within literary and elite circles may have, in the long run, a cascading effect to other social strata. The English-language national press does occasionally voice viewpoints alternative to the mainstream pro-English discourse. In a letter to the *New Straits Times*, for example, a reader vigorously challenged the myth of the *orang putih* (white man) as 'expert' and explained that hiring foreign teachers of English purely on the basis of their being foreign was very unwise. The reader reported of a foreign English language officer who "had been hired to advise and train teachers" even if "his background was neither in English language teaching nor education," "he had never stepped into a primary or secondary school classroom" and "[t]he only training he had was a three-month course in teaching English." The reader ended the letter by making the point that English is not owned by, and need not be associated to, any one particular nationality:

> English is an international language. No one owns it. We do not need to speak in a British, an American or an Australian accent to get ourselves understood. As long as we speak and use standard English competently, we are intelligible to the world. The same should apply to all English language teachers – qualified and competent language users – no matter if English is their first language or not.
>
> ("Foreigners not the solution", 2009)

While opinions such as the one above still represent rare voices out of the choir, it remains to be seen whether they might become more common with time.

7
The Relocation of English

...I SPEAK ONLY ENGLISH!
I don't speak England...

—zekrypton (a user in an online forum)

7.1 Introduction

The picture that emerges from the discussion that has unfolded in this book so far is one where two antithetic narratives about the relocation of English run along parallel lines: the academic discourse narrative and the public discourse narrative. On the one hand, the academic discourse narrative tells of an English language that has been transplanted in different parts of the world and describes the ways in which this linguistic re-rooting has been accompanied by local processes of acculturation. It also describes how these, in turn, have given rise to varieties of English that have reached different levels of development, stabilisation and recognition. On the other hand, the public discourse narrative tells of an English language that, because of its worldwide diffusion, is constantly under threat of corruption by the negative influence of local languages and cultures. One sees the acculturation and consequent diversification of English as a positive and necessary phenomenon producing beneficial liberatory effects for its users, while the other sees it as counterproductive and detrimental to the effectiveness of global communication.

In this chapter I argue that this difference is only apparent and that the two positions are actually two expressions of the same essentialist conceptualisation of the English language. Subsequently, I make the case that the study of EIW is best approached from an entirely non-linguistic point of view so that the relocation of English is considered not a matter of linguistic form but one of linguistic re-balance, both on the world stage and within each individual's linguistic repertoire.

7.2 Focus on form

One point in common between the academic discourse narrative and the public discourse narrative is that both are concerned with the sounds, the lexis, the grammar, the syntax and the pragmatics of EIW. In particular, they are interested in the ways in which these deviate from the norms of what Wierzbicka (2006) calls 'Anglo English'. As was seen in Chapter 6, in Malaysia, the dominant discourse portrays the local use of English as being marred by an unrelenting process of deterioration. This decline in quality is considered to be directly proportional to the perceived degree of localisation of the English language. In other words, the more English appears to have a Malaysian character, the more it is considered corrupted, flawed, broken or a *rojak*. And so the public discourse stresses the importance of conserving a 'pure' form of English, faithful to its Anglosaxon ancestral roots. Linguists in the field of EIW focus on exactly the same thing, the *rojak*, albeit from a different perspective. They tend to see the relocation of English fundamentally in terms of the degree to which nativised, localised and acculturised forms of English differ from the norms of 'Inner-Circle' English. And so the questions raised both in the public discourse and in the academic field of EIW are essentially the same: How and why does English vary in the world? How and why do the different varieties deviate from the original form? What is the level of development, recognition and codification that these varieties have reached? Which English is most suitable for people to learn and use?

In fact, *bahasa rojak* and 'pure' English are conceptually equivalent sides of the same coin. The idea that there is a 'rotten' form of English entails the possibility that there exists a pure form too. The notion of the diversification of English and its pluralisation into Englishes assumes that somewhere there must be a singular, non-diverse form of it: no matter what attitude one has about the causes or the consequences of it, deviation requires norm. As Wierzbicka notes, "arguably, it is this Anglo English that provides a point of reference for all the other Englishes, one without which the notion of Englishes would not make sense either" (2006, p. 9). If world Englishes and English as a lingua franca are *variations of* English, it means that they are *not* the 'original' English. Therefore, even if a case is made and accepted that distinctive features are to be seen as markers of the legitimate acculturation of English in new sociocultural realities or of the function of it as a lingua franca, the foundations of the centralist and/or purist position are not really undermined but reinforced. The focus on form, therefore, prevents any discussion about the relocation of English from going very far.

Indeed, it can be said that emphasis on the linguistic aspects of EIW can not only restrict but also invalidate the whole notion of relocation. Wierzbicka, for example, argues that common English words such as *reasonable, right, wrong, fair* and *probably* are inextricably part, and expression, of the 'Anglo' cultural heritage embedded in the English language and, following a Humboldtian conception of language, claims that this shows "how unrealistic the slogan 'yes to English and no to Anglo cultural values' really is" (2006, p. 312). The idea that the *language* English is, inevitably, the expression of the *culture* English can be taken forward and used, as Robert Phillipson (1992, 2003, 2008, 2009) does, to corroborate the hypothesis that the spread of English may be a form of Anglo-American imperialism. According to the 'linguistic imperialism' theory, English is not only the property of Wierzbicka's 'Anglo' speakers, but also a vehicle by which such speakers impose their own interests onto the rest of the world. Significantly, despite the evidently non-linguistic repercussions, the theory, at its core, still makes explicit references to bare-bone linguistics:

> English is not a space. It is a piece of real estate. Its owners – whose biological identities keep changing, as in the case of any real estate, – enforce normative spelling, punctuation, grammar, and phonological and lexical limits (within which accents and dictions may vary) throughout the domains of English discourse. Indian use of English will forever remain a tolerated, degenerate variant of the norm in the eyes of the owners.
>
> (Dasgupta, 1993, p. 203, cited in Phillipson, 2008)

Indeed, the citation above encapsulates one of the main concepts that I have discussed in this book and makes evident how a focus on form, whether aimed at denigrating or lauding variety, draws very strong demarcation lines encircling, at one time, the 'real estate' English, 'Anglo' culture and the 'Inner Circle'. It forbids the relocation of English. My contention, therefore, is that the notion of relocation cannot be cultivated on the terrain of language form.

Manifestly, the concerns within the academic field of EIW have followed an agenda "not always directly connected with linguistics" (Hickey, 2004, p. 505). After all, as Pennycook notes, "[w]hen we talk of

English today we mean many things, and not many of them to do with some core notion of language" (Pennycook, 2006, p. 112). The result is that the aims of the study of EIW have generally been a hybrid of linguistics and sociopolitical preoccupations. More precisely, it can be said that linguistic analysis has underpinned positions that are primarily ideological. Some scholars are uncomfortable with the mix and are openly against locating the study of EIW within non-linguistic agendas. Notably, Schneider considers it essential that work on the development of postcolonial Englishes be kept free of political preoccupations:

> Personally, I strongly believe that we should try to keep scholarly investigation separate, as far as reasonably possible, from taking a political stand: the evolution of language follows principles of its own, and a preconceived mind, set upon pursuing some sociopolitical agenda, is likely to be barred from recognizing such principles, directing one's attention elsewhere.
>
> (Schneider, 2007, p. 19)

Whether or not one agrees with Schneider, the question he poses needs to be taken seriously. But the question I wish to ask is specular to Schneider's: should EIW be studied entirely in terms of its sociopolitical significance, without regard to its linguistic aspects? The answer depends largely on how one considers the whole notion of 'language'.

7.3   Dislodging linguistics

Bolton (2006b) has observed that there is "a tension between what are seen as the organic qualities of dialects and varieties as the 'natural' expression of vital linguistic systems, and the view of languages and language varieties as social and political constructs" (p. 308). Within this dualism, in the field of EIW there seems to be a certain propensity towards the former conception of language. This is because much of the rubric in both the World Englishes and the ELF research areas is ontological, given that a great deal of attention is devoted to proving the existence of linguistic entities such as nativised varieties of English and English as a lingua franca. Scholars in these fields have made efforts to identify different manifestations of EIW and to qualify them by means of descriptions of their 'organic qualities'. The various national (*Singaporean, Indian*, etc.) and functional (*lingua franca*) names find justification in the proven existence of the objects they are attached to. From this point of view, the study of EIW would seem to operate on essentialist ground, whereby names denote, and are a consequence of, objects of reality. The researcher-linguist's task is then to identify each object-language, to describe it as accurately as possible and give it a suitable and unique name.

This naming practice corresponds to what is described as the 'causal theory of reference', according to which "a term refers to whatever it is causally linked to in a certain way" while "[t]hese links do not require speakers to have beliefs about the referent" (Devitt and Sterelny, 1999, p. 66). Within this theory, names are created to designate objects that exist irrespective and *a priori* of those names:

> The name is introduced at a formal or informal dubbing. This dubbing is in the presence of an object that will from then on be the bearer of the name. The event is perceived by the dubber and probably others. To perceive something is to be causally affected by it. As a result of this causal action, a witness to the dubbing, if of suitable linguistic sophistication, will gain an ability to use the name to designate the object. Any use of the name exercising that ability designates the object in virtue of the use's causal link to the object: perception of the object prompted the thoughts which led to the use of the name. In short, those present at the dubbing acquire a semantic ability that is causally grounded in the object.
>
> (1999, pp. 66–67)

If this concept is applied to the domain of descriptive linguistics, the linguist can be seen as the dubber of object-languages. The problem is that linguists often take an epistemological shortcut by making use of pre-existing, ready-made names. So they are no longer the original dubbers but merely the borrowers of names, that is, "[p]eople not at the dubbing [who] acquire the semantic ability from those at the dubbing" (Devitt and Sterelny, 1999, p. 67). But, as discussed in Chapter 2, the dubbing of languages is often political and its purpose is precisely to *appear* to be consequent of a genuine case of causal link between objects and names, as part of broader national narratives seeking to prove the ancient historical roots of nations. So, in their position of borrowers, or 'people not at the dubbing', linguists have limited or no control over the accuracy of the names they use. Consequently, this seems to irrecoverably invalidate any supposition of scientific rigour in attempts to distinguish languages from one another if such attempts rely on those borrowed names.

Significantly, Chomsky, who has always advocated a scientific approach to the study of language, is wary of the "crucial sociopolitical dimension" and is not content with "the commonsense notion of language" that it produces: "We speak of Dutch and German as two separate languages, although some dialects of German are very close to dialects that we call 'Dutch' and are not mutually intelligible with others that we call 'German'" (1986, p. 15). And, indeed, one of the parameters commonly utilised in attempting to distinguish languages from one another objectively is precisely that of mutual intelligibility. The *Ethnologue*, for example, is a project which aims to categorise the languages of the world in the most rigorous possible way and, according to its editor Barbara Grimes, "the criterion for listing speech varieties separately is low intelligibility, as far as that can be ascertained" (Grimes, 2000). However, immediate questions arise. How exactly can intelligibility be 'ascertained'? What is the precise cut-off point of intelligibility below which two 'speech varieties' can be considered separate languages? Is intelligibility dependent on formal linguistic features or on individual speakers' capacity or willingness to understand each other? A number of scholars reject the validity of this parameter altogether. Joseph, for example, states categorically that

> the question of what is or isn't a language is always finally a *political* question. The linguist cannot answer it objectively by measuring degrees of structural differences or mutual comprehensibility.
>
> (Joseph, 2006, p. 27)

As Hudson notes, "[m]utual intelligibility is a matter of degrees" and that it is "not really a relation between varieties, but between people, since it is they, and not the varieties, that understand one another" (1996, p. 35). He then comes to the conclusion that "the search for language boundaries is a waste of time" (1996, p. 36) and that "there is no way of delimiting varieties, and we must therefore conclude that varieties do not exist. All that exists are people and items, and people may be more or less similar in the items they have in their language" (1996, p. 39). The boundaries between national languages are linguistically much fuzzier than the political borders delimiting one country from its neighbours. The names of the languages people say they speak depend on the national groups they wish to identify themselves with. And this is far more important than any attempt to categorise languages scientifically, which is not only a fruitless exercise but also ultimately inconsequential:

what does it matter if a few thousand linguists are convinced that Serbian and Croatian are the same language, or that Chinese is a family of distinct languages, when umpteen millions believe the opposite, and it's on their lives that the question has a direct impact?

(Joseph, 2006, p. 26)

Sydney Lamb has a virtually identical position about the absence of objective criteria for the distinction of languages: "There is no generally applicable way to make the distinction between one language and another. Languages are neither discrete objects nor are they uniform across speakers" (2004, p. 413). For Lamb, names of languages do not denote objects of reality, but the reverse relationship can nonetheless be activated. That is, the coinage of such names establishes and codifies the existence of the entities they purport to describe:

[...] any time you have a noun you assume that there must be some thing, some kind of object that that noun is a representation of. We have a noun "language" and so we assume, without ever giving much thought to it, that there is such a thing as a language and that it is some kind of an object. But the more you think about it, the more you realize that there is no such object. There is no such thing as a language. There is such a thing as Language, but it is a mass noun.

(Lamb, 2004. p. 218)

The non-existence of uniform languages or varieties implies that each individual speaker uses a uniquely different variety. This concept applies, of course, to varieties of English too:

Now we know that there are distinct varieties of English – many syntactic differences have been discussed that distinguish American from British English. And various regional syntactic differences within the United States or within the United Kingdom are well known. But what if it turned out that for every single pair of English speakers [...] one could find at least one clear syntactic difference?

My own experience in observing the syntax of English speakers [...] makes me think that it is entirely likely that no two speakers of English have exactly the same syntactic judgements. In which case there must be many more varieties of English than is usually assumed. In fact, if it is true than no two English speakers have the same (syntactic) grammar, then the number of varieties of English

[…] must be at least as great as the number of native speakers of English.

(Kayne, 2000, p. 8)

If Kayne can be excused for limiting the scope of his observation to 'native speakers', linguistically, this is the only conclusion that can be reached.

If languages and varieties are social and political constructs, Pennycook, if rather sceptically, hints at "the phenomenological argument that languages exist only to the extent that speakers perceive them to do so" (2006, p. 95). Indeed, as Joseph notes, "[s]o long as people *believe* that their way of speaking constitutes a language in its own right, there is a real sense in which it *is* a real language" (2006, p. 27). Significantly, even the *Ethnologue* has to concede that "[s]ociological criteria such as the speakers' views concerning the relationship between language and identity, and between language and political or geographic factors, are also important" (Grimes, 2000), implicitly confirming the constructionist view of languages. So, if such constructionist view is accepted, the attention devoted in the study of EIW to distinct linguistic features which supposedly characterise varieties of English and/or ELF appears to be irrelevant. It is for this reason that I maintain that the relocation of English cannot be studied in terms of language form but in terms of what people are prepared to do with this entity that they, without doubt, call English.

7.4   The relocation of English: A concrete example

Qatar's Al Jazeera is currently one of the largest international TV networks in the world. Originally an Arabic-only news channel, it has had a dramatic expansion in recent years. It became known to a much wider audience in the immediate aftermath of the "September 11" attacks, when it broadcast video and audio messages purportedly from Al-Qaeda. Partly because it was seen as Al-Qaeda's preferred vehicle for their messages to the outer world, Al Jazeera began to establish itself as a news channel with its own marked non-Western identity and as an alternative to global networks like CNN or BBC World. The popularity of the news channel continued to grow in the following years, to the point that in November 2006 Al Jazeera decided to launch a new channel: Al Jazeera English.

The name was significant. So much so that until one day before its official launch, the channel was to be called Al Jazeera International, and it was only in a last-minute decision that it was finally named Al Jazeera English. According to the online version of the *Guardian* newspaper,

> the late change came about because one of the Qatar-based channel's backers decided that the broadcaster already had an international scope with its original Arabic outlet and that the new offering should be named after the language it is broadcast in.
>
> (Holmwood, 2006)

So, on the surface, the name change from *International* to *English* was a switch from a geographical emphasis to a linguistic emphasis. However, deeper meanings and connotations lie right beneath that surface. First of all, it is clear that an expansion of the channel's geographical reach was the fundamental reason to create the new Al Jazeera channel. The obvious linguistic reference in the word *English* was not for its own sake: the choice of English was undoubtedly dictated by the worldwide spread of that language rather than by any particular affection for it. So, in effect, while Al Jazeera was already an international news channel, the ability to broadcast in English would make it much more than just international – it would make it *global*. As its own website states, Al Jazeera English is "the world's first global English language news channel to be headquartered in the Middle East". Here, "global" and "English language" collocate very closely, and one is to be taken as the natural consequence of the other.

It is within this global mapping of the English language, with no precise points of reference or coordinates, that the notion of *location* becomes crucial. Specifically, the fact that Al Jazeera's headquarters are located in the Middle East is particularly significant:

> From this unique position, Al Jazeera English is destined to be the English-language channel of reference for Middle Eastern events, balancing the current typical information flow by reporting from the developing world back to the West and from the southern to the northern hemisphere.
>
> (Al Jazeera English website)

What is unique about the position of Al Jazeera English? This is an example where the literal meaning of "position" illustrates perfectly well its derived metaphorical meaning and where both meanings are indeed relevant. From a literal point of view, "position" refers to a physical place, and the uniqueness of Al Jazeera English is given by its geographical location: an English-language TV news channel reaching every corner of the world from its Middle Eastern base is unique. As the website says, this enables Al Jazeera English to counter the flow of information which normally travels from north to south or from the Developed World to the Developing World. The concepts of 'north' and 'Developed World' are actually too broad here. The major global TV news networks are American (CNN and CNBC) and British (BBC World). It would be therefore more accurate to use the expression 'Anglophone West' to refer to the source of the normal information flow. Again, this can be understood in a physical/geographical sense, as Figure 7.1 and Figure 7.2 illustrate.

The geographical mapping of this idea of 'information counterflow' can be translated into its closely derived figurative meaning, so that the position of Al Jazeera English is not just a physical one but also a political and ideological one. Inverting the direction of the information flow equates to offering alternative viewpoints on the same events recounted and, ultimately, on the world. And indeed,

> The channel aims to give voice to untold stories, promote debate, and challenge established perceptions.
>
> (Al Jazeera English website)

Al Jazeera exemplifies an important step towards a redefinition of the coordinates of English, as the primary stated aim of using this language is that of "providing a unique grassroots perspective from under-reported regions around the world to a potential global audience of over one billion English speakers" (Al Jazeera English website). This is, in principle, very similar to the postcolonial literary phenomenon of 'writing back' (Ashcroft et al., 1989), whereby Caribbean, African and Asian writers wrote about their own settings from their own perspectives, seeking to rebalance the one-way flow of literary representations of the Orient that for centuries had been coming from the Occident. One key common element in both Al Jazeera English and the 'writing back' movement is the use of the English language as the vehicle for this "contrapuntal reading" (Said, 1993) of established perceptions.

Figure 7.1   Information flow from the Anglophone West to the rest of the world

Figure 7.2   Information counterflow

Crucially, while the Anglophone West begins to lose its status both as the sole source of global dissemination of information and as the exclusive rights holder to established views of the world, the language through which such views have been traditionally expressed also begins to be used to offer alternative perspectives. This scenario prefigures the necessity to reformulate the relocation of English.

7.5 The relocation of English: The SCIP model

The now traditional view in the academic field of EIW is that non-Anglo Englishes are in a position to challenge the supposed superiority of Anglo English:

> The imperial centre brought English to the distant colonies of the periphery. Now these postcolonial nations not only bring new Englishes to the monolingual Anglophones, but are contesting their power to authorise English and its teaching. The emergence of these new Englishes challenges long held assumptions about the value of standardised UK, US, or Australian Englishes [...].
>
> (Singh et al., 2002, p. 26)

What I have contended in this book is that the real challenge is of a different nature. The relocation of English begins with the loosening of the knot that ties the English language to what Holliday (1994) calls BANA (Britain, Australasia and North America), namely, the first phase of a process involving four interconnected types of transition, as shown in Figure 7.3. First of all, the physical spread of English in the world

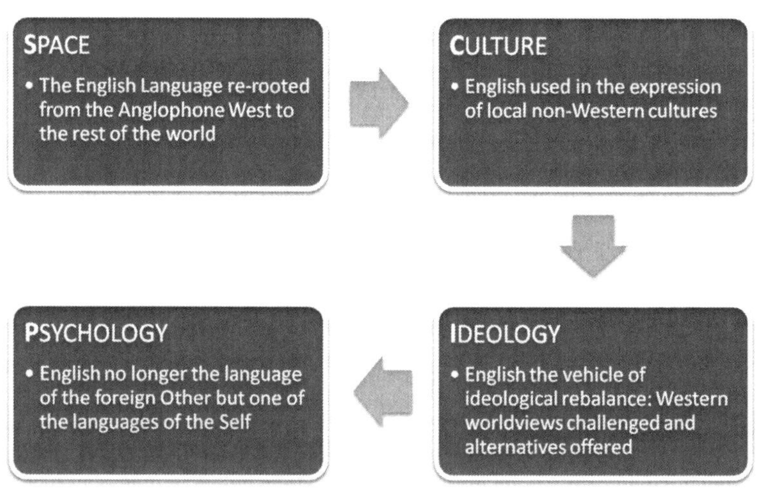

Figure 7.3 The relocation of English: The SCIP model

causes the re-rooting of the language. In turn, this gives rise to a phenomenon whereby, in the first instance, various local cultures find new forms of expression through English and, subsequently, the scope of this phenomenon broadens beyond the confines of local settings and offers alternative views of the world to those emanating from the Anglophone West. The process continues until these alternative perspectives become sufficiently established and the English language becomes instrumental to a re-balance of the ideological flows in the world and plays a central role in countering the possibility of the ideological and cultural domination of one group over everybody else. The relocation culminates when English ceases to be somebody else's language, or the language of the Other, and can truly and comfortably become one of the Self's languages.

A few decades ago Nigerian writer Chinua Achebe said that the language of his creative writing had to be able to "carry the weight of [his] African experience" and, therefore, needed to be a "new English, still *in full communion with its ancestral home* but altered to suit its new African surroundings" (Achebe, 1965, p. 30, my emphasis). The bottom line of this book is that that communion is no longer necessary. This entity that we call English, like all other forms of language, has no ancestral home. Each individual speaker uses it in ways that suit their surroundings, be them that of home, air traffic control or online blogging. There is no need of a programmatic alteration of English. The relocation of English is realised not so much by authorising a plurality of new Englishes, but by treating English as a language that can carry and share the weight of a plurality of experiences, worldviews and inner thoughts with a multitude of groups and individuals who are willing to take part in the sharing.

References

Abas, A. and H. Hamid (9 August 2009) DPM: Vital to boost English proficiency. *New Straits Times*. Retrieved 27 August 2009, from http://www.nst.com.my/Current_News/NST/articles/8xks/Article/index_html.

Abraham, C.E.R. (2006) *Speaking Out: Insights into Contemporary Malaysian Issues*. Kuala Lumpur: Utusan Publications.

Achebe, C. (1965) English and the African writer. *Transition*, 18, 27–30.

Anderson, B. (1991) *Imagined Communities: Reflections on the Origin and Spread of Nationalism* (2nd Edition). London: Verso.

Annamalai, E. (2005) Nation-Building in a Globalised World: Language Choice and Education in India. In Lin, A.M.Y. and P.W. Martin (eds) *Decolonisation, Globalisation: Language-in-Education Policy and Practice*. Clevedon: Multilingual Matters, pp. 20–37.

Anyidoho, A. and M.E. Dakubu (2008) Ghana: Indigenous Languages, English, and an Emerging National Identity. In Simpson, A. (ed.) *Language and National Identity in Africa*. Oxford: Oxford University Press, pp. 141–157.

Ashcroft, B., G. Griffiths and H. Tiffin (1989) *The Empire Writes Back: Theory and Practice in Post-Colonial Literatures*. London: Routledge.

Audit first (14 July 2009) *New Straits Times*. Retrieved 28 August 2009, from http://www.nst.com.my/Current_News/NST/articles/20090714074949/Article/.

Azmi, D. (21 June 2009) Our unifying mother tongue. *The Star*. Retrieved 28 August 2009, from http://thestar.com.my/columnists/story.asp?file=/2009/6/21/columnists/contradictheory/4128035&sec=Contradictheory.

Bamgboṣe, A. (1982) Standard Nigerian English: Issues of Identification. In Kachru, B. (ed.) *The Other Tongue*. Urbana: University of Illinois Press, pp. 99–111.

Bamgboṣe, A. (1995) Ethnic Englishes in Nigeria: The role of literature in the development of Igbo English. *Journal of Cultural Studies*, 2(1), 219–230.

Bamgboṣe, A. (1997) English in the Nigerian Environment. In Bamgbose, A., A. Banjo and A. Thomas (eds) *New Englishes: A West African Perspective*. Trenton, NJ: Africa World Press, pp. 9–26.

Bamgboṣe, A. (1998) Torn Between the norms: Innovations in world Englishes. *World Englishes*, 17(1), 1–14.

Bamgboṣe, A. (2001) World Englishes and globalization. *World Englishes*, 20(3), 357–363.

Becker, H.S. (1963) *Outsiders: Studies in the Sociology of Deviance*. New York: The Free Press.

Benson, P. (2005) Chinese Englishes: A sociolinguistic history (book review). *English Language and Linguistics*, 9(2), 377–381.

Berns, M. (2009) English as lingua franca and English in Europe. *World Englishes*, 28(2), 192–199.

Bhabha, H.K. (1990) Introduction: Narrating the Nation. In Bhabha, H.K. (ed.) *Nation and Narration*. London: Routledge, pp. 1–7.

Bhabha, H.K. (1994) *The Location of Culture*. London: Routledge.

Bilingualism is the way to go (21 June 2009) *The Star*. Retrieved 27 August 2009, from http://thestar.com.my/news/story.asp?file=/2009/6/21/education/4150215&sec=education.

Bisong, J. (1995) Language choice and cultural imperialism: A Nigerian perspective. *ELT Journal*, 49(2), 122–132.

Boehmer, E. (2005) *Colonial and Postcolonial Literature: Migrant Metaphors*. Oxford: Oxford University Press.

Bokhorst-Heng, W.D., L. Alsagoff, L. Mckay and R. Rubdy (2007) English language ownership among Singaporean Malays: Going beyond the NS/NNS dichotomy. *World Englishes*, 26(4), 424–445.

Bolton, K. (2003) *Chinese Englishes*. Cambridge: Cambridge University Press.

Bolton, K. (2006a) World Englishes Today. In Kachru, B.B., Y. Kachru and C.L. Nelson (eds) *The Handbook of World Englishes*. Oxford: Blackwell, pp. 240–269.

Bolton, K. (2006b) Varieties of World Englishes. In Kachru, B.B., Y. Kachru and C.L. Nelson (eds) *The Handbook of World Englishes*. Oxford: Blackwell, pp. 289–312.

Bring the fun back to the teaching of English (11 July 2009) *New Straits Times*. Retrieved 28 August 2009, from http://www.nst.com.my/Current_News/NST/articles/17johan0710/Article/index_html.

Bruthiaux, P. (2003) Squaring the circles: Issues in modeling English worldwide. *International Journal of Applied Linguistics*, 13(2), 159–178.

Brutt-Griffler, J. (2002) *World English: A Study of Its Development*. Clevedon: Multilingual Matters.

Brutt-Griffler, J. and K.K. Samimy (2001) Transcending the nativeness paradigm. *World Englishes*, 20(1), 99–106.

Burchfield, R. (1985) *The English Language*. Oxford: Oxford University Press.

Canagarajah, S. (1999) *Resisting Linguistic Imperialism in English Teaching*. Oxford: Oxford University Press.

Canagarajah, S. (2007) Lingua Franca English, multilingual communities, and language acquisition. *The Modern Language Journal*, 91(1), 923–939.

Cavallaro, F. and Ng, B.C. (2009) Between status and solidarity in Singapore. *World Englishes*, 28(2), 143–159.

Chomsky, N. (1965) *Aspects of the Theory of Syntax*. Boston: MIT Press.

Chomsky, N. (1986) *Knowledge of Language: Its Nature, Origin and Use*. New York: Praeger.

Clarify English status (20 July 2009) *New Straits Times*. Retrieved 29 August 2009, from http://tst.nst.com.my:8080/Current_News/NST/articles/19PPSM/Article/index_html.

Cogo, A. (2008) English as a lingua franca: Form follows function. *English Today*, 24(3), 58–61.

Cogo, A. and M. Dewey (2006) Efficiency in ELF communication: From pragmatic motives to lexico-grammatical innovation. *Nordic Journal of English Studies*, 5(2), 59–94.

Collin, F. (1997) *Social Reality*. London: Routledge.

Crystal, D. (1997/2003) *English as a Global Language*. Cambridge: Cambridge University Press.

Crystal, D. (2001) The Future of Englishes. In Burns, A. and C. Coffin (eds) *Analysing English in a Global Context*. London: Routledge, pp. 53–64.

Dasgupta, P. (1993) *The Otherness of English: India's Auntie Tongue Syndrome.* New Delhi: Sage.

Davies, A. (1991) *The Native Speaker in Applied Linguistics.* Edinburgh: Edinburgh University Press.

Davies, A. (1996) Review article: Ironising the myth of linguicism. *Journal of Multilingual and Multicultural Development,* 17(6), 485–596.

Davies, A. (2003) *The Native Speaker: Myth and Reality.* Clevedon: Multilingual Matters.

Davies, A. (2004) The Native Speaker in Applied Linguistics. In Davies, A. and C. Elder (eds) *The Handbook of Applied Linguistics.* Oxford: Blackwell, pp. 431–450.

Deterding, D. and A. Kirkpatrick (2006) Emerging South-East Asian Englishes and intelligibility. *World Englishes,* 25(3/4), 391–409.

Devitt, M. and K. Sterelny (1999) *Language and Reality.* Oxford: Blackwell.

Dewey, M. (2007) English as a lingua franca and globalization: An interconnected perspective. *International Journal of Applied Linguistics,* 17(3), 332–354.

Discourage use of 'lah' in English (11 February 2009) *The Star.* Retrieved 27 August 2009, from http://thestar.com.my/news/story.asp?file=/2009/2/11/focus/3241660&sec=focus.

English can help breach 'international barrier' (12 June 2009) *The Star.* Retrieved 27 August 2009, from http://thestar.com.my/news/story.asp?file=/2009/6/12/focus/4099299&sec=focus.

English can help launch Malaysia to next level of growth (16 July 2009) *The Star.* Retrieved 27 August 2009, from http://biz.thestar.com.my/news/story.asp?file=/2009/7/16/business/4328487&sec=business.

English for maths and science (13 July 2009) *The Star Online: Blog.* Retrieved 28 August 2009, from http://blog.thestar.com.my/permalink.asp?cat=21&id=24828.

Even China banking on English (12 June 2009) *The Star.* Retrieved 29 August 2009, from http://thestar.com.my/news/story.asp?file=/2009/6/12/focus/4091055&sec=focus.

Fanon, F. (1967) *Black Skin, White Masks.* New York: Grove Press.

Ferguson, C.A. (1982) Foreword. In Kachru, B.B. (ed.) *The Other Tongue: English Across Cultures.* Urbana, IL: University of Illinois Press, vii–xi.

Foo, B. and Richards, C. (2004) English in Malaysia. *RELC Journal,* 35(2), 229–240.

Foreigners not the solution (14 July 2009) *New Straits Times.* Retrieved 29 August 2009, from http://www.nst.com.my/Current_News/NST/articles/18engt/Article/index_html.

Gaudart, H. (1987) English Language Teaching in Malaysia: A historical account. *The English Teacher, XVI.* Retrieved 28 August 2009, from http://www.melta.org.my/ET/1987/main2.html.

Get students started on the basics (21 August 2009) *New Straits Times.* Retrieved 28 August 2009, from http://www.nst.com.my/Current_News/NST/articles/18tiche/Article/index_html.

Giddens, A. (2002) *Runaway World: How Globalisation Is Reshaping Our Lives* (2nd Edition). London: Profile Books.

Give them a choice of schools (16 July 2009) *New Straits Times.* Retrieved 28 August 2009, from http://www.nst.com.my/Current_News/NST/articles/18englang/Article/.

Görlach, M. (1991) *Englishes*. Amsterdam: John Benjamins.

Görlach, M. (1995) *More Englishes*. Amsterdam: John Benjamins.

Görlach, M. (1998) *Even More Englishes*. Amsterdam: John Benjamins.

Görlach, M. (2002) *Still More Englishes*. Amsterdam: John Benjamins.

Graddol, D. (1997) *The Future of English?* London: British Council.

Graddol, D. (2006) *English Next*. London: British Council.

Grammar drilling will help weak students (2 July 2009) *The Star*. Retrieved 27 August 2009, from http://thestar.com.my/news/story.asp?file=/2009/7/2/focus/4215228&sec=focus.

Grimes, B.F. (2000) *Ethnologue 14*. http://www.ethnologue.com.

Halliday, M.A.K. (1978) *Language as Social Semiotic: The Social Interpretation of Language and Meaning*. London: Edward Arnold.

Halliday, M.A.K. (1985/1994) *An Introduction to Functional Grammar*. London: Edward Arnold.

Halliday, M.A.K. and C.M.I.M. Matthiessen (2004) *An Introduction to Functional Grammar* (3rd Edition). London: Edward Arnold.

Halliday, M.A.K., A. McIntosh and P.D. Strevens (1964) *The Linguistic Sciences and Language Teaching*. London: Longmans.

Harris, R. (2001) Linguistics after Saussure. In Cobley, P. (ed.) *Semiotics and Linguistics*. London: Routledge, pp. 118–133.

Heng, C.S. and H. Tan (2006) English for mathematics and science: Current Malaysian language-in-education policies and practices. *Language and Education*, 20(4), 306–321.

Herb, G.H. and D.H. Kaplan (eds) (1999) *Nested Identities: Nationalism, Territory and Scale*. Lanham, MD: Rowman and Littlefield.

Hickey, R. (2004) Englishes in Asia and Africa: Origin and Structure. In Hickey, R. (ed.) *Legacies of Colonial English: Studies in Transported Dialects*. Cambridge: Cambridge University Press, pp. 503–535.

Higgins, C. (2003) 'Ownership' of English in the outer circle: An alternative to the NS-NNS Dichotomy. *TESOL Quarterly*, 37(4), 615–644.

Hitchings, H. (2008) *The Secret Life of Words*. New York: Farrar, Straus and Giroux.

Hobsbawm, E.J. (1992) *Nations and Nationalism since 1780: Programme, Myth, Reality*. Cambridge: Cambridge University Press.

Hodge, R. and G. Kress (1988) *Social Semiotics*. Cambridge: Polity.

Holborrow, M. (1999) *The Politics of English: A Marxist View of Language*. London: Sage.

Holliday, A. (1994) *Appropriate Methodology and Social Context*. Cambridge: Cambridge University Press.

Holmwood, L. (2006) Al-Jazeera renames English-language channel. *guardian.co.uk* Retrieved 1 September 2009, from http://www.guardian.co.uk/media/2006/nov/14/tvnews.television1.

Honey, R.D. (1999) Territory and Identity in Precolonial Nigeria. In Herb, G.H. and D.H. Kaplan (eds) *Nested Identities: Nationalism, Territory and Scale*. Lanham, MD: Rowman and Littlefield, pp. 175–198.

House, J. (2009) Introduction: The pragmatics of English as a lingua franca. *Intercultural Pragmatics*, 6(2), 141–145.

How do I get rid of my accent? (5 March 2009) *The Star*. Retrieved 29 August 2009, from http://thestar.com.my/lifestyle/story.asp?file=/2009/3/5/lifefocus/3280165&sec=lifefocus.

HRH Raja Zarith Sofia Idris (2009) Royal Lecture. MELTA International Conference (Johor Bahru, 11–13 June 2009).

Hudson, R.A. (1996) *Sociolinguistics* (2nd Edition). Cambridge: Cambridge University Press.

If you fail English, no SPM certificate (9 June 2009) *The Star Online: Blog.* Retrieved 28 August 2009, from http://blog.thestar.com.my/permalink.asp?id=24025.

Innes, C.L. (2007) *The Cambridge Introduction to Postcolonial Literatures in English.* Cambridge: Cambridge University Press.

It's the teachers who are failing us (18 August 2009) *New Straits Times.* Retrieved 28 August 2009, from http://www.nst.com.my/Current_News/NST/articles/19GLI/Article/index_html.

Jenkins, J. (2000) *The Phonology of English as an International Language.* Oxford: Oxford University Press.

Jenkins, J. (2002) A sociolinguistically based, empirically researched pronunciation syllabus for English as an international language. *Applied Linguistics,* 23(1), 83–103.

Jenkins, J. (2003) *World Englishes: A Resource Book for Students.* London: Routledge.

Jenkins, J. (2006a) Global Intelligibility and Local Diversity: Possibility or Paradox? In Rubdy, R. and M. Saraceni (eds) *English in the World: Global Rules, Global Roles.* London: Continuum, pp. 32–39.

Jenkins, J. (2006b) Current perspectives on teaching world Englishes and English as a lingua franca. *TESOL Quarterly,* 40(1), 157–181.

Jenkins, J. (2007) *English as a Lingua Franca: Interpretations and Attitudes.* Oxford: Oxford University Press.

Jenkins, J. (2009) Exploring Attitudes towards English as a Lingua Franca in the East Asian Context. In Murata, K. and J. Jenkins (eds) *Global Englishes in Asian Contexts.* Basingstoke: Palgrave Macmillan, pp. 40–58.

Joned, S.B. (1994) *As I Please: Selected Writings 1975–1994.* London: Skoob Books.

Joseph, J.E. (2004) *Language and Identity: National, Ethnic, Religious.* Basingstoke: Palgrave Macmillan.

Joseph, J.E. (2006) *Language and Politics.* Edinburgh: Edinburgh University Press.

Kachru, B.B. (1976) Models of English for the third world: White man's linguistic burden or language pragmatics? *TESOL Quarterly,* 10(2), 221–239.

Kachru, B.B. (1981) The Pragmatics of Non-native Varieties of English. In Smith, L. (ed.) *English for Cross-Cultural Communication.* Basingstoke: Palgrave Macmillan, pp. 15–39.

Kachru, B.B. (1982) Models for Non-native Englishes. In Kachru, B.B. (ed.) *The Other Tongue: English across Cultures.* Urbana, IL: University of Illinois Press, pp. 325–350.

Kachru, B.B. (1985) Standard, Codification and Sociolinguistic Realism: The English Language in the Outer Circle. In Quirk, R. and H.G. Widdowson (eds) *English in the World: Teaching and Learning the Language and Literatures.* Cambridge: Cambridge University Press, pp. 11–30.

Kachru, B.B. (1986) *The Alchemy of English.* Oxford: Pergamon.

Kachru, B.B. (1988a) The Spread of English and Sacred Linguistic Cows. In Lowenberg, P.H. (ed.) *Language Spread and Language Policy: Issues, Implications and Case Studies.* Washington, DC: Georgetown University Press, pp. 207–228.

Kachru, B.B. (1988b) The sacred cows of English. *English Today,* 4(4), 3–8.

Kachru, B.B. (1991) Liberation linguistics and the Quirk concern. *English Today*, 7(1), 3–13.

Kachru, B.B. (1996) Norms, Models and Identities. *The Language Teacher Online*, 20(10). Retrieved from http://jalt-publications.org/tlt/files/96/oct/englishes. html.

Kachru, B.B. (2005) *Asian Englishes*. Hong Kong: Hong Kong University Press.

Kachru, B.B. (2009) Asian Englishes in the Asian Age: Contexts and Challenges. In Murata, K. and J. Jenkins (eds) *Global Englishes in Asian Contexts: Current and Future Debates*. Basingstoke: Palgrave Macmillan, pp. 175–193.

Kachru, B.B. and L. Smith (1985) Editorial. *World Englishes*, 4(2), 209–212.

Kachru, Y. and L. Smith (2008) *Cultures, Contexts, and World Englishes*. London: Routledge.

Kayne, R.S. (2000) *Parameters and Universals*. Cambridge, MA: MIT Press.

Kirkpatrick, A. (2006) Which Model of English: Native Speaker, Nativised or Lingua Franca? In Rubdy, R. and M. Saraceni (eds) *English in the World: Global Rules, Global Roles*. London: Continuum, pp. 71–83.

Kirkpatrick, A. (2007a) *World Englishes: Implications for International Communication and English Language Teaching*. Cambridge: Cambridge University Press.

Kirkpatrick, A. (2007b) Linguistic Imperialism? English as a Global Language. In Hellinger, M. and A. Pauwels (eds) *Handbook of Language and Communication: Diversity and Change*. Berlin: Mouton de Gruyter, pp. 333–364.

Kirkpatrick, A. (2008) English as the official language of ASEAN: Features and strategies. *English Today*, 24(2), 27–34.

Kloss, H. (1967) 'Abstand Languages' and 'Ausbau Languages'. *Anthropological Linguistics*, 9(7), 29–41.

Krishnaswamy, N. and A.S. Burde (1998) *The Politics of Indians' English*. Oxford: Oxford University Press.

Kumaravadivelu, B. (2003) A postmethod perspective on English language teaching. *World Englishes*, 22(4), 539–550.

Lamb, S.M. (2004) *Language and Reality*. London: Continuum.

Link, B.G. and J.C. Phelan (2001) Conceptualizing stigma. *Annual Review of Sociology*, 27, 363–385.

Mahathir, M. (1999) *A New Deal for Asia*. Petaling Jaya: Pelanduk Publications.

Mandal, S.K. (2000) Reconsidering cultural globalization: The English language in Malaysia. *Third World Quarterly*, 21(6), 1001–1012.

Manglish spanner in the works (29 July 2009) *New Straits Times*. Retrieved 27 August 2009, from http://www.nst.com.my/Current_News/NST/articles/18enli/Article/index_html.

Matsuda, A. (2002) Symposium on world Englishes and teaching English as a foreign language: Introduction. *World Englishes*, 21(3), 420.

McArthur, T. (1987) The English Language or the English Languages? In Bolton, W.F. and D. Crystal (eds) *The English Language*. London: Sphere, pp. 323–341.

McArthur, T. (2002) *The Oxford Guide to World English*. Oxford: Oxford University Press.

McColl Millarf, R. (2005) *Language, Nation and Power*. Basingstoke: Palgrave Macmillan.

McLean, W. (1946) Education in Malaya. *The Journal of Negro Education*, 15(3), 508–512.

Medgyes, P. (1992) Native or non-native: Who's worth more? *ELT Journal*, 46(4), 340–349.

Mehrotra, R.R. (1998) *Indian English: Texts and Interpretations*. Amsterdam: John Benjamins.

Mesthrie, R. and R.M. Bhatt (2008) *World Englishes: The Study of New Linguistic Varieties*. Cambridge: Cambridge University Press.

Ngũgĩ wa Thiong'o (1986) *Decolonising the Mind*. London: Heinemann.

No doubting BM's relevance (28 August 2009) *New Straits Times*. Retrieved 28 August 2009, from http://www.nst.com.my/articles/19teaah/Article/index_html.

Okara, G. (1963) African Speech … English words. *Transition*, 3(10), 15–16.

Omar, A.H. (1992) *The Linguistic Scenery in Malaysia*. Kuala Lumpur: Dewan Bahasa dan Pustaka. Retrieved 29 August 2009, from http://openlibrary.org/b/OL1386497M/linguistic-scenery-in-Malaysia.

Omar, A.H. (1994) English in Malaysia: A Typology of Its Status and Roles. In Kandiah, T. and J.K. Terry (eds) *English Language Planning: A Southeast Asian Contribution*. Singapore: Times Academic Press, pp. 242–260.

On making a pass in English compulsory in SPM (11 June 2009) *The Star Online: Blog*. Retrieved 28 August 2009, from http://blog.thestar.com.my/permalink.asp?id=24094.

Only in Malaysia (8 July 2009) *The Star*. Retrieved 27 August 2009, from http://thestar.com.my/english/story.asp?file=/2009/7/8/lifefocus/4140107&sec=lifefocus.

Open up more English schools (12 July 2009) *The Star*. Retrieved 27 August 2009, from http://thestar.com.my/news/story.asp?file=/2009/7/12/education/4288579&sec=education.

Pakir, A. (2009) English as a lingua franca: Analyzing research frameworks in international English, world Englishes, and ELF. *World Englishes*, 28(2), 224–235.

Pandian, A. (2002) English language teaching in Malaysia today. *Asia Pacific Journal of Education*, 22(2), 35.

Parakrama, A. (1995) *De-Hegemonizing Language Standards: Learning from (Post)colonial Englishes about "English"*. London: Macmillan.

Pennycook, A. (1994) *The Cultural Politics of English as an International Language*. London: Longman.

Pennycook, A. (1998) *English and the Discourses of Colonialism*. London: Routledge.

Pennycook, A. (2003) Global Englishes, Rip Slyme, and performativity. *Journal of Sociolinguistics*, 7(4), 513–533.

Pennycook, A. (2006) *Global Englishes*. London: Routledge.

Pennycook, A. (2009) Plurilithic Englishes: Towards a 3D Model. In Murata, K. and J. Jenkins (eds) *Global Englishes in Asian Contexts: Current and Future Debates*. Basingstoke: Palgrave Macmillan, pp. 194–207.

Phillipson, R. (1992) *Linguistic Imperialism*. Oxford: Oxford University Press.

Phillipson, R. (2003) *English-only Europe?* London: Routledge.

Phillipson, R. (2008) Lingua franca or lingua frankensteinia? English in European integration and globalisation. *World Englishes*, 27(2), 250–267.

Phillipson, R. (2009) *Linguistic Imperialism Continued*. London: Routledge.

Platt, J., H. Weber and M.L. Ho (1984) *The New Englishes*. London: Routledge and Keagan Paul.

PPSMI wajib dimansuh (11 June 2009) *Utusan Malaysia Online – Pendidikan*. Retrieved 31 August 2009, from http://www.utusan.com.my/utusan/info.asp?y=2009&dt=0611&pub=Utusan_Malaysia&sec=Pendidikan&pg=pe_05.htm.

Prator, C.H. (1968) The British heresy in TESL. In Fishman, J.A., C.A. Ferguson and J. Das Gupta (eds) *Language Problems of Developing Nations*, London: Wiley, pp. 459–476.

Prodromou, L. (2007) Is ELF a variety of English? *English Today*, 23(2), 47–53.

Quirk, R. (1985) The English Language in a Global Context. In Quirk, R. and H.G. Widdowson (eds) *English in the World: Teaching and Learning the Language and Literatures*. Cambridge: Cambridge University Press, pp. 1–6.

Rajagopalan, K. (1997) Linguistics and the myth of nativity: Comments on the controversy over 'new/non-native Englishes'. *Journal of Pragmatics*, 27(2), 225–231.

Rajagopalan, K. (1999) Of EFL teachers, conscience and cowardice. *ELT Journal*, 53(3), 200–206.

Ramanathan, V. (2005) *The English-Vernacular Divide*. Clevedon: Multilingual Matters.

Rampton, M.B.H. (1990) Displacing the 'native speaker': Expertise, affiliation, and inheritance. *ELT Journal*, 44(2), 97–101.

Rao, R. (1938) *Kanthapura*. London: Allen and Unwin.

Rubdy, R. and M. Saraceni (2006) Introduction. In Rubdy, R. and M. Saraceni (eds) *English in the World: Global Rules, Global Roles*. London: Continuum, pp. 5–16.

Rubdy, R., S. McKay, L. Alsagoff and W. Bokhorst-Heng (2008) Enacting English language ownership in the outer circle: A study of Singaporean Indians' orientations to English norms. *World Englishes*, 27(1), 40–67.

Rushdie, S. (1997) Introduction. In Rushdie, S. and E. West (eds) *The Vintage Book of Indian Writing: 1947–1997*. London: Vintage, pp. ix–xxii.

Said, E. (1978) *Orientalism*. New York: Pantheon Books.

Said, E. (1993) *Culture and Imperialism*. London: Chatto and Windus.

Saraceni, M. (2008) English as a lingua franca: Between form and function. *English Today*, 24(2), 20–26.

Savignon, S. (2003) Teaching English as communication: A global perspective. *World Englishes*, 22(1), 55–66.

Saville-Troike, M. (1996) The Ethnography of Communication. In McKay, S.L. and N.H. Hornberger (eds) *Sociolinguistics and Language Teaching*. Cambridge: Cambridge University Press, pp. 351–382.

Say, it will be nice if we aren't proud of Manglish (25 July 2009) *The Star*. Retrieved 27 August 2009, from http://thestar.com.my/news/story.asp?file=/2009/7/25/focus/4388380&sec=focus.

Schneider, E.W. (2003) The dynamics of new Englishes: From identity construction to dialect birth. *Language*, 79(2), 233–281.

Schneider, E.W. (2007) *Postcolonial English: Varieties Around the World*. Cambridge: Cambridge University Press.

Seidlhofer, B. (2001) Closing a conceptual gap: The case for a description of English as a lingua franca. *Journal of Applied Linguistics*, 11(2), 133–158.

Seidlhofer, B. (2005) English as a lingua franca. *ELT Journal*, 59(4), 339–341.

Seidlhofer, B. (2006) English as a Lingua Franca in the Expanding Circle: What It Isn't. In Rubdy, R. and M. Saraceni (eds) *English in the World: Global Rules, Global Roles*. London: Continuum, pp. 40–50.

Seidlhofer, B. (2009) Common ground and different realities: World Englishes and English as a lingua franca. *World Englishes*, 28(2), 236–245.

Seidlhofer, B. and J. Jenkins (2003) English as a Lingua Franca and the Politics of Property. In Mair, C. (ed.) *The Politics of English as a World Language*. Amsterdam: Rodopi, pp. 138–156.

Seidlhofer, B. and H.G. Widdowson (2009) Accommodation and the Idiom Principle in English as a Lingua Franca. In Murata, K. and J. Jenkins (eds) *Global Englishes in Asian Contexts: Current and Future Debates*. Basingstoke: Palgrave Macmillan, pp. 26–39.

Seton-Watson, H. (1977) *Nations and States: An Enquiry into the Origins of Nations and the Politics*. London: Taylor and Francis.

Simply the language of the world (22 June 2009) *New Straits Times*. Retrieved 28 August 2009, from http://www.nst.com.my/Current_News/NST/articles/19bahas/Article/.

Singh, M., P. Kell and A. Pandian (2002) *Appropriating English: Innovation in the Global Business of English Language Teaching*. New York: Peter Lang.

Smith, L.E. (1976) English as an international auxiliary language. *RELC Journal*, 7(2), 38–42.

Talib, I. (2002) *The Language of Postcolonial Literatures: An Introduction*. London: Routledge.

Tan, P.K.W. (1999) Speech presentation in Singaporean English novels. *World Englishes*, 18(3), 359–372.

Tan, P.K.W. (2005) The medium-of-instruction debate in Malaysia: English as a Malaysian language? *Language Problems & Language Planning*, 29(1), 47–66.

Taylor, D. (1995) What Do EFL Teachers Need to Know about Pronunciation? In Lewis, J.W. (ed.) *Studies in General and English Phonetics*. London: Routledge, pp. 454–463.

Trudgill, P. (2003) *A Glossary of Sociolinguistics*. Edinburgh: Edinburgh University Press.

Trudgill, P. (2004) *New-Dialect Formation. The Inevitability of Colonial Englishes*. Edinburgh: Edinburgh University Press.

Trudgill, P. and J. Hanna (1982) *International English: A Guide to Varieties of Standard English*. London: Edward Arnold.

Tupas, R. (2006) Standard Englishes, Pedagogical Paradigms and Their Conditions of (Im)possibility. In Rubdy, R. and M. Saraceni (eds) *English in the World: Global Rules, Global Roles*. London: Continuum, pp. 169–185.

Walder, D. (1998) *Post-Colonial Literatures in English: History, Language, Theory*. Oxford: Blackwell.

Webster, N. (1783) *A Grammatical Institute of the English Language. Part I*. Hartford: Hudson and Goodwin.

Webster, N. (1789) *Dissertations on the English Language*. Boston: Isaiah Thomas.

Well-educated but not literate in English (30 June 2009) *The Star*. Retrieved 29 August 2009, from http://thestar.com.my/news/story.asp?file=/2009/6/30/focus/4219331&sec=focus.

What's the question again? (13 February 2009) *The Star*. Retrieved 27 August 2009, from http://thestar.com.my/lifestyle/story.asp?file=/2009/2/13/lifefocus/3238673&sec=lifefocus.

What's there to boast when we're speaking Manglish? (21 July 2009) *The Star*. Retrieved 27 August 2009, from http://thestar.com.my/news/story.asp?file=/2009/7/21/focus/4355461&sec=focus.

Why the need to go English (19 June 2009) *The Star*. Retrieved 27 August 2009, from http://thestar.com.my/news/story.asp?file=/2009/6/19/focus/20090619065520&sec=focus.

Widdowson, H.G. (1994) The ownership of English. *TESOL Quarterly*, 28(2), 377–389.

Widdowson, H.G. (1998) EIL: Squaring the circles. A reply. *World Englishes*, 17(3), 397–401.

Wierzbicka, A. (2006) *English: Meaning and Culture*. Oxford: Oxford University Press.

Wong, C.W. (12 July 2009) A poor legacy for our kids. *The Star*. Retrieved 28 August 2009, from http://thestar.com.my/columnists/story.asp?file=/2009/7/12/columnists/onthebeat/4304574&sec=On%20The%20Beat.

Wright, S. (2000) *Community and Communication: The Role of Language in Nation State Building and European Integration*. Clevedon: Multilingual Matters.

Wright, S. (2004) *Language Policy and Language Planning*. Basingstoke: Palgrave Macmillan.

Yano, Y. (2001) World Englishes in 2000 and beyond. *World Englishes*, 20(2), 119–131.

Yano, Y. (2009) The Future of English: Beyond the Kachruvian Three Circle Model? In Murata, K. and J. Jenkins (eds) *Global Englishes in Asian Contexts: Current and Future Debates*. Basingstoke: Palgrave Macmillan, pp. 208–225.

Index